'*Take My Yoke* is a delight. It h
insight on every page. If you ne
of God's great love, then this is
Dr Fred Drummond, Head of Pra

'In a world of increasing uncertainty, spiritual rest is an antidote to the demands of modern society. In Chic's thoughtful and practical book, he explores the journey of rest, which is both a place of arrival and destination, it is an ongoing experience of encounter and growth. We never become experts but learn afresh every day. I particularly enjoyed the use of way markers and how grace-filled they are. I highly encourage all of us on the journey to benefit from the lived experience shared in this book.'
Scott Brennan, a Guardian of the Community of Aidan and Hild

'I have known Chic for twenty-nine years. One thing, among many characteristics, that stands out about him is how hard a worker he is. It was, then, striking and impressive to discover that *Take My Yoke* is a liberating life's work of confronting himself and the faith story handed down to him. He exposes an existential problem of faith: the syndrome of always reverting to shouldering burdens that Jesus never asked us to pick up. Contending against the incessant, unrewarding strain of effort, Chic recasts another way of living the faith through the complementary motifs of rest, jubilee, grace and the coming new creation. *Take My Yoke* bravely takes a fresh biblical look at Jesus' offer to take the weight from our weary backs to show us a way forward into freedom.'
Stuart Weir, Head of CARE for Scotland

'This is not just a book about the theory of practice but the practice of theory. At a time when there is much talk about intimacy with God and the embrace of divine love, Chic Lidstone examines, explores and exemplifies this from his own

experience. *Take My Yoke* intermingles closely examined biblical exposition with deeply personal descriptions of encountering the God of Scripture in daily life. Chic shares with us his rich reflection on many years of Christian discipleship. Humbly and honestly, he allows Scripture to speak into his experience and generously shares with us his own discoveries. The simple practices at the end of each section are personal invitations to try out the contemplative quietness of soul that the book describes.'
Martin Hodson, General Director, Baptist Union Scotland

'This book is a breath of fresh air for anyone weary from the endless striving to prove their worth. With gentle clarity and compassion, Chic invites us to lay down the burdens of performance and perfection, and to look to the cross – where Jesus has already done it all. In a culture that tells us love must be earned and rest must be deserved, this book offers a liberating message of grace: we bring nothing, yet everything has been freely given. It's not a dense theological work, but a heartfelt call to true freedom – the kind that comes not from doing more, but from resting in what's already been done. If your soul longs for peace, rest and a lighter way, this might just be your turning point.'
Dr Elaine Matthews (GP)

Cover design: John Halvorsen, BDes (hons).

Take My Yoke

Chic Lidstone

instant apostle

First published in Great Britain in 2025

Instant Apostle
104A The Drive
Rickmansworth
Herts
WD3 4DU

Copyright © Chic Lidstone 2025

The author has asserted his rights under Section 77 of the Copyright, Designs and Patents Act, 1988, to be identified as the author of the work.

Cover design John Halvorsen, BDes (hons).

All rights reserved. No portion of this book may be reproduced or transmitted in any form or by any means, electronic or mechanical, including photocopying and recording, or by any information storage and retrieval system, without permission in writing from the publisher.

Unless otherwise indicated, all Scripture quotations are taken from the Holy Bible, New International Version® Anglicised, NIV® Copyright © 1979, 1984, 2011 by Biblica, Inc.® Used by permission. All rights reserved worldwide.

Scripture quotations marked 'RSV' are taken from the Revised Standard Version of the Bible, copyright © 1946, 1952, and 1971 the Division of Christian Education of the National Council of the Churches of Christ in the United States of America. Used by permission. All rights reserved.

Scripture quotations marked 'NLT' are taken from the Holy Bible, New Living Translation, copyright © 1996, 2004, 2015 by Tyndale House Foundation. Used by permission of Tyndale House Publishers, Inc., Carol Stream, Illinois 60188. All rights reserved.

Scripture quotations marked 'NASB' are taken from the New American Standard Bible®. Copyright © 1960, 1962, 1963, 1968, 1971, 1972, 1973, 1975, 1977, 1995 by The Lockman Foundation. Used by permission.

Scripture quotations marked 'ESV' are from the ESV® Bible (The Holy Bible, English Standard Version®), copyright © 2001 by Crossway, a publishing ministry of Good News Publishers. Used by permission. All rights reserved.

Scripture quotations marked 'KJV' are taken from the Authorized (King James) Version. Rights in the Authorized Version in the United Kingdom are vested in the Crown. Reproduced by permission of the Crown's patentee, Cambridge University Press.

Scripture quotations marked 'NKJV' are taken from the New King James Version®. Copyright © 1982 by Thomas Nelson. Used by permission. All rights reserved.

Scripture quotations marked 'CSB' are taken from the Christian Standard Bible. Copyright © 2017 by Holman Bible Publishers. Used by permission. Christian Standard Bible®, and CSB® are federally registered trademarks of Holman Bible Publishers, all rights reserved.

Scripture quotations marked 'The Message' are from The Message. Copyright © 1993, 1994, 1995, 1996, 2000, 2001, 2002. Used by permission of NavPress Publishing Group.

Every effort has been made to seek permission to use copyright material reproduced in this book. The publisher apologises for those cases where permission might not have been sought and, if notified, will formally seek permission at the earliest opportunity.

The views and opinions expressed in this work are those of the author and do not necessarily reflect the views and opinions of the publisher.

British Library Cataloguing-in-Publication Data

A catalogue record for this book is available from the British Library.

This book and all other Instant Apostle books are available from Instant Apostle:

Website: www.instantapostle.com

Email: info@instantapostle.com

ISBN 978-1-912726-94-3

Printed in Great Britain.

For Issie, my wife, who has journeyed with me
in our life of faith.

Jesus' yoke is not an instrument of subjugation but a means of liberation.
Eder Ferraz[1]

---

[1] Used by permission.

Contents

Preface: Who is this for?.. 11
Introduction: Setting the scene... 13
1: A journey into rest 16
2: Come!... 23
3: Time for something new 26
4: A traditional understanding.. 44
5: The gift 58
6: Jesus' yoke 74
7: Through the Old Testament 99
8: Rest in creation 126
9: A big picture 142
10: Today!.. 158
11: Practical rest... 168
12: Cycle of grace 182
13: In my end is my beginning... 190
14: A new story... 196
Appendix 203

Preface
Who is this for?

Life is not measured by the number of breaths we take, but by the moments that take our breath away.
Vicki Corona[2]

This book is for those who need to have their breath taken away by a fresh revelation of God's love. In writing these pages I have had moments when I experienced that and was moved to tears. By God's goodness, I pray this will also be your experience.

It is for those 'ordinary' Christians, although there is no such thing, who need a fresh revelation of who Jesus is and what this life of faith is about, or rather, who it is about.

It is for those leaders who need a fresh experience of joy, who need to be reminded of the calling that they originally knew and that they were willing to give their lives for Jesus and His Church, but who may have grown cold.

For whatever reason, our life of faith may have lost its sparkle, and we are challenged by the gap between the life promised and the current reality. Many feel 'short

---

[2] Attributed to Vicki Corona. www.goodreads.com/topic/show/785932-origin-of-quote-life-is-not-measured-by-the-number-of-breaths-we-take (accessed 3rd April 2025)

changed', although few may admit that we have become jaded and that our once vibrant faith now feels more like a cold, lifeless duty. Fresh oxygen needs to be breathed into lives of faith to make it once again that promised life-changing and joy-filled experience. Many are leaving the Church, not because they have lost their faith in God, but because they have lost their faith in Church.

If this resonates with you, I pray that you may find a fresh understanding of the life-giving reality of Jesus' words again or for the first time.

Introduction
Setting the scene

Blessed are those whose strength is in you,
whose hearts are set on pilgrimage.
Psalm 84:5

We are familiar with the term 'hardening of the arteries' as a medical problem that can increase the chance of a stroke or heart attack. But how many of us have considered that we may be suffering from hardening of the *'ought-eries'*? Hardening of the 'ought-eries' refers to a life dominated by a relentless sense of obligation – constantly feeling the need to meet expectations, whether our own, others' or even, we may believe, God's. To live with this condition is to be continually plagued by the relentless thought, 'Whatever I do is never enough.' It may not lead to a heart attack, but can so often affect our heart of hearts, which may lead to (among other symptoms) depression, burnout or simply turning away from faith, because 'it is just too hard'.

This condition can happen because we have a poor understanding of who we are in Christ and a poor understanding of what God actually wants from us and, importantly, what He wants for us.

The words of Jesus speak directly into this situation of being driven:

> Come to me, all you who are weary and burdened, and I will give you rest. Take my yoke upon you and learn from me, for I am gentle and humble in heart, and you will find rest for your souls. For my yoke is easy and my burden is light.
> (Matthew 11:28-30)

Many know this passage well and are familiar with what it is like to be driven, and yet find it hard to equate the two! Now that I am aware of this, I find that many scriptures actually address it; however this is the obvious one, so I will start here.

The Message Bible paraphrases the passage in its own unique and often helpful style:

> Are you tired? Worn out? Burned out on religion? Come to me. Get away with me and you'll recover your life. I'll show you how to take a real rest. Walk with me and work with me – watch how I do it. Learn the unforced rhythms of grace. I won't lay anything heavy or ill-fitting on you. Keep company with me and you'll learn to live freely and lightly.

Exploring what Jesus meant by these words will shed new light on our understanding of this passage, taking it from our heads to our hearts, as at the core of this Jesus is speaking to our heart of hearts. Bringing rest for our souls, and healing for our 'hardened ought-eries'.

Using this book

This is book is a journey, from Jesus heralding a new era to a magnificent revelation of grace at the end, in which I invite you to join me. Recently, my wife, some friends and I walked the Fife Pilgrim Way in Scotland. Along the route, waymarkers encouraged us to keep going, guided us and provided moments to pause and reflect. One such point was the church at Markinch, which over countless centuries has been used as a resting place for pilgrims. As we sat outside the church, breathing fresh air in the sunshine, it was good to rest, eating our packed lunch and reflecting on what we had seen and learned. In a similar way, at the end of each section of this book, you will find a 'waymarker', encouraging you to pause and to review what has been learned and where on the journey you are. As you walk with me, I hope that your hardened 'oughteries' will ease and you will again breathe fresh air in the sunshine of God's grace.

I do not see myself as an academic or a theologian but as a practitioner who has endeavoured to live out my Christian faith in many different areas, so please don't expect a polished theological document. Rather, see it as a journey, which I trust is biblically grounded, helping us all grasp in a deeper way what this life of faith looks like.

Over the years, I have read widely. While I will reference sources where possible, much of what I share has been shaped by personal study and lived experience that has simply formed who I am and what I believe.

1
A journey into rest

> Religion is not the church we go to but the cosmos we live in.
> Our world and our culture are in the greatest need of rest, and peace for our souls.
> G K Chesterton[3]

My own journey of learning

A close friend recently asked me, 'After all your years in industry, leadership and preaching, why do you want to write about this?'

On reflection, I came to the conclusion that in many ways this defines my own story. I think this addressed an unrelenting need in my own life, but also one that is pressing in many of our lives, in the Church and also in our increasingly fast-paced world. As I have begun to share my heart on this, I find that I am not alone, with many saying that it strikes a deeply resonant note. Out of all the things I have learned and preached, this still touches me more deeply than anything else.

---

[3] Cited in Richard Rohr, *The Universal Christ*, London: SPCK, 2019, p6.

Let me explain

Years ago, at a Bible week in a tent on yet another rainy Scottish summer's evening, when worship was beautiful and deeply moving, I asked God to be close and embrace me. The answer that came back was clear and shocking: 'No.' That set me on a journey which later I realised I had been on for a long time.

Many years before that night in the tent, during a stressful time as a civil engineer, I was running several contracts and working long hours travelling crazy distances each day. Life had become intolerable and exhausting. It felt as though I was on a hamster wheel that I could not get off. Previously I felt that the Lord had promised that my work would be worship, but at this precise time that seemed a million miles away. In hindsight, I realise that God was working deeply in my life, calling me further into Him and towards church leadership.

As I drove those long and at times lonely miles across Scotland, I would sometimes be so overwhelmed by God's love that I had to stop the car and simply let myself be embraced by Him. I recall one particular time on an early summer morning high above Loch Lomond when I was praying as I drove to yet another stress-filled day at work. I was overcome by such a presence of the Lord in the car that I had to pull over and stop. I don't know how long I sat there, unable to pray and hardly even able to breathe as the Lord was so close. Time stood still and eventually I had to ask the Lord to let me go as I was struggling to breathe! I knew the Lord was with me and that He loved me! I don't know whether it was a response to stress or a deep spiritual encounter, but it was undeniably real to me in that moment.

Later, after leaving my career as an engineer and embarking on a new direction of church leadership, I would again be overwhelmed by the magnitude of the task God had called me to and, again, I would have to pull over and yield to what felt like a very physical embrace. As before, I had to ask the Lord to stop as I simply could not breathe!

Going back to that night in the tent when I felt the shock of the Lord saying, 'No,' I had to go outside and sort it out with God! My wife will often sense a leading to a certain chapter and verse without knowing exactly what the verse is about; it is often appropriate to the occasion. I don't normally work that way, but that evening I had a strong sense that I should look at Matthew 23:37:

> Jerusalem, Jerusalem, you who kill the prophets and stone those sent to you, how often I have longed to gather your children together, as a hen gathers her chicks under her wings, and you were not willing.

I was stunned! The Lord had called me by name from Scripture – 'Chic' (OK, I know the spelling is not precise)! But I felt the Lord saying, 'Chic, I would embrace you, but you are too busy so I can't.' As you can imagine, that stopped me in my tracks, and so a long period of reflection and interior work started.

I began to explore a more contemplative way of being. As you will have gathered by now, I am out-and-out activity driven, so I found this hard, but essential. I started to read different kinds of books which I would describe as 'how to be', as well as the more technical 'how to do' books on church leadership. I began to learn how to simply sit in the presence of the Lord and listen. I was introduced to the work of the Northumbria Community,[4] which reacquainted me with the 'art' of sitting and contemplation. I learned to sit for fifteen or twenty minutes of a morning in the Lord's presence. Just sitting, not praying, not studying, but simply sitting and giving room for Him to speak, to be with me and me with Him.

As part of this, I use a reflective practice which has helped me many times, personally and in leading individuals and groups. This is how it goes; maybe you would like to try it sometime.

Finding a quiet space, I pray, asking the Holy Spirit to guide me, then I imagine a scene from around AD30, when I am leaving Jerusalem, with the city gates behind me. I begin to walk. I see a campfire over to my right in a bit of scrubland, around which there is a group of a dozen or so people, and then I recognise Jesus among the group. Asking the Holy Spirit to guide, I then consider and imagine what to do next. I occasionally repeat this exercise as and when I feel the need to, and each time I have a different experience, which often helps me understand what God wants to say to me.

The first time I did this, I recall looking at my watch (I know it is AD30 and watches were not invented then, but stay with me!) and thinking, 'I don't have time for this but I know I need to go over, I can't not.' So I simply went over

---

[4] www.northumbriacommunity.org (accessed 6th March 2025).

and joined the group. The most telling part was my nervous glance at my watch.

Sometime later, I did the same exercise, asking the Holy Spirit to guide me through the scenario again, and this time as I went over, Jesus was very clearly telling me to be quiet and sit down, pointing to a log on His left. I sat down, while Jesus remained standing, and I just sat. Very soon after, I contracted shingles, resulting in taking time off work and being forced to 'sit down'! Lovely people wanted to pray for healing and a quick recovery back to activity. I welcomed the prayer but declined the offer of a quick return to activity as I knew I was where I was meant to be, with God having things to teach me. During this time, which lasted a few months, I journeyed through Henri Nouwen's wonderful book, *The Return of the Prodigal*.[5] For months I 'sat on that log' as I listened to the Lord and read that book.

My health recovered and life was good as the church grew and I was seeing fruit in my ministry. However, sometime later, things again began to get difficult, so I made time to visit a trusted Christian counsellor, with whom I had to do some further hard work. She unravelled that I was suffering from that 'hardening of the oughteries', which I referred to earlier. My life was driven by the thoughts of 'I ought to do this and ought to do that'; in effect I was driven, to the point where I was damaging my health and no doubt the lives of those closest to me. I won't go any deeper into the drivers causing this, as I think we

---

[5] Henri Nouwen, *The Return of the Prodigal: A Story of Homecoming*, London: Darton, Longman & Todd, 2004.

all have different ones and it will not add anything to list mine.

Again, more time off work as the Lord worked deeply within me. I was returned to health as I relearned what it is to sit still and allow Him to embrace me. After going through the spiritual exercise described above again, I heard Jesus say, 'Lean closer and let Me embrace you.' This was very difficult indeed, as I have a skin condition from birth which makes embrace uncomfortable, and the thought of itchy, scratchy robes around me was physically off-putting. Not surprisingly, that resulted in a reflective interior journey until I was willing and even hungered for that embrace, robes and all!

I was getting desperate. When was I ever going to get off this 'log' and get on with ministry? When I finally felt the Lord say it was time to get up, He showed me that I was not to go alone but, in fact, it would be a dance, a dance with Jesus. Sure, getting up and moving, but in that dynamic embrace with Him. Ken Gire's book *The Divine Embrace*[6] helped me to see this.

During one of these times of reflection, I remember an evening at a local restaurant with my wife. As I savoured a particularly delicious lamb shank, I recall hearing God whisper, 'What do you want, really want, in your heart of hearts?' That did take me by surprise, and I thought about it for a few moments and asked the Lord if He could give me time to think and reflect on it. It was much too big a question to answer spontaneously, and anyway, the lamb shank was so delicious!

---

[6] Ken Gire, *The Divine Embrace*, Carol Stream, IL: Tyndale House Publishers, 2003.

I prayed, thought and reflected on this for some months and eventually, in reading through the Psalms, I found that Psalm 27 echoed my decision:

> One thing I ask from the LORD,
> this only do I seek:
> that I may dwell in the house of the LORD
> all the days of my life,
> to gaze on the beauty of the LORD
> and to seek him in his temple …
> My heart says of you, 'Seek his face!'
> Your face, LORD, I will seek.
> Do not hide your face from me.
> (Psalm 27:4, 8-9)

Have I learned this lesson? Am I living in this perfect divine embrace? I would love to say yes, but that would not be truthful. I try to, and sometimes am better at it than at other times, but it is something I hunger for and I know what it feels like. It is something to press into and return to in greater depth to reset myself when things get hard. I am beginning to recognise those drivers that rob me of peace, telling me to work harder, and I have learned to say no. But this is not a one-time thing; it is a lifetime of work.

One day, when I'm fully embraced in His love, I will know rest as I never have before. Until then, I press on, knowing that His embrace is always within reach and that this is a lifelong journey.

I hope that, by being honest and sharing my journey, I can encourage you to find that promised rest for your own soul.

2
Come!

> The journey of a thousand miles begins with one step.
> *Lao Tzu*[7]

Jesus is a master at conveying deep truths in simple and profound ways. His teachings and parables are like small but powerful grace-filled explosives that are easy to swallow but then burst inside you! These bursts of grace can and will radically change your life if you let them.

This is the case with these simple, beautiful words of Jesus:

> Come to me, all you who are weary and burdened, and I will give you rest. Take my yoke upon you and learn from me, for I am gentle and humble in heart, and you will find rest for your souls. For my yoke is easy and my burden is light.
> (Matthew 11:28-30)

When you let these words truly sink in, their riches and grace-filled power will transform your life. They may

---

[7] www.brainyquote.com/quotes/lao_tzu_137141 (accessed 5th April 2025).

stretch you, they may reduce you to tears or make you laugh with joy, but I hope and pray they will change your life as they have mine. Are you ready?

These powerful words from Jesus are part of a larger narrative of God's people seeking rest and a deeper relationship with Him. The Songs of Ascent, for instance, from Psalms 120 to 134, provide a picture of this kind of journey and are traditionally understood as a suite of psalms used by pilgrims on their journey to festival celebrations in Jerusalem. The first song starts with the idea that the psalmist was hungering for a deeper reality and integrity of faith than he was currently experiencing. He resolves to acknowledge his dissatisfaction and sets out on a journey to a deeper and more satisfying experience and reality of faith. The subsequent psalms map this journey and destination.

On this journey we'll begin with Jesus' promise of rest in Matthew, exploring how the words 'Come to me' invite us into a deeper reality of faith. Along the way, we will visit many different themes and passages which may help us understand ourselves and our faith better, as well as encourage us to comprehend what these wonderful words of Jesus can mean.

Similar to the Psalms of Ascent and my pilgrimage experience I talked of earlier, you will find at the end of each chapter an opportunity to pause and reflect on your journey into the Father's embrace.

So let's get started!

Waymarker

Sit
Sit quietly in a place where you feel safe, and quieten your heart. When you are settled, invite the Holy Spirit to guide you. Remain in that place, listening to your heart.

Reflect
If God were to ask you, 'What is your heart longing for?', what would you say? What is your deepest desire?

Psalm 120 talks about the psalmist's dissatisfaction with where he is and he cries out to God to save him. In contrast, Psalm 121 changes the tone to one that speaks of a place of security and peace. Violence and deceit may not be the culture that you are crying to God to save you from, but you can ask God to reveal what is on your heart and why He has brought you to this place.

Pray
Bring what comes to your mind and heart before God. He already knows your heart and is present with you in this place. He is your refuge.

And so, as in Psalm 120, this journey begins!

3
Time for something new

> See, I am doing a new thing!
> Now it springs up; do you not perceive it?
> I am making a way in the wilderness
> and streams in the wasteland.
> *Isaiah 43:19*

The wonderful invitation of Jesus, to come to Him and rest, heralds a profound shift in the way of knowing God. Jesus, as recorded by Matthew, carefully places this invitation in a wider context, clearly saying that the former ways of understanding and practising faith have come to an end, making room for a new approach to knowing God as Father and experiencing His loving embrace.

In this chapter we will look at the passage from Matthew 11:2 to 12:14, unfolding the narrative that is the immediate context in which these words have been carefully placed. Matthew 11:2–12:14 is like a framework where verses 11:28-30 form the central truth holding the surrounding passage together – without wishing to be flippant, much like the filling in a sandwich.

John the Baptist: Matthew 11:2-19

No matter how hard we try, we inevitably view Scripture through the lens of our own experience. That is entirely normal, but something we should be aware of and, accordingly, make a conscious effort to consider other views, especially those of people we respect but who think differently.

At the beginning of chapter 11 we find John in prison and obviously having doubts about Jesus being the Messiah. We don't condemn him for this, but respect him for taking steps to resolve his deepest fears by reaching out to Jesus; fears that he may have got it wrong all along and devoted his life to something and Someone he had once been so sure of. Rather than remain in a vortex of doubt, which is a dark place that many of us may be acquainted with, he sends a message to Jesus for reassurance.

Jesus in turn sends back an encouraging message to John that what he sees happening is actually in keeping with what was prophesied for the Messiah. John just needs help to see this again. In a dark place he has become confused, but Jesus encourages him to stay the course.

The predominant thinking of the day that John was possibly falling back into was, of course, that the Messiah would throw off the heavy yoke of foreign domination and that Israel would once again be a sovereign state under the rule of God, with a descendant of David on the throne as king.

John did not see this happening and so was questioning what was going on and what Jesus was doing. God through Jesus, however, was using another route than the expected one of conquering and overcoming through the usual means of power – military, political, economic and religious, etc. Instead, through sacrifice and disarming the very powers, both human and spiritual, by allowing them to do their worst by killing His Son, God was drawing the full sting of evil's underlying power and conquering by nullifying it, thus proving it inadequate.[8]

The different positions of human power are well documented. The Pharisees thought that a more righteous life would please God, causing the Messiah to come and release Israel from Roman tyranny.

The Essenes lived in the desert and were the creators of the Dead Sea Scrolls. They thought that withdrawing from the politics and corruption in Jerusalem and living a secluded monastic life was the answer to the pressing problems of the day. From this place in the wilderness they could engage as they chose with society, as John the Baptist may have been doing. It was possible that he was an Essene.

The Zealots were all for the violent overthrow of the occupying Roman forces, and we learn that even among Jesus' disciples was Simon the Zealot.

The Sadducees, who were the ruling class and temple-focused elite, got on with the business of cooperating with the Roman forces so that the temple could keep running, and no doubt their pockets lined.

John had heard reports about what Jesus was doing and, as we have seen, it was not what he had expected. He was anticipating fire, like the prophet Elijah in his violent encounter with the prophets of Baal, recorded in 1 Kings 18. He was anticipating a Messiah who would stand up to

---

[8] N T Wright, *Evil and The Justice of God*, Downers Grove, IL: IVP, 2006.

Herod and overthrow the Romans. Crucially, he was expecting to be released, as the Messiah was meant to set the captives free.

However, God's ideas were different, calling sinners to repentance and radical obedience, not through fear or condemnation as was the way of the religious leaders, but through loving and valuing. In caring, Jesus never condoned the sin but valued the person highly, something which religion and society had not done. The religious elite considered that anyone who did not live up to their strict religious and ritual codes was the root of the problem that Israel was facing, while Jesus began to make it clear that actually it was the other way around! John understood this, but needed reassurance, which made him ask the question, 'Are you the one who is to come, or should we expect someone else?' (v3). Jesus, as He often did, took this question and used it as an opportunity to go deeper and further than the question itself was asking.

He turned to the crowds and began to talk to them in a different and unexpected way about John, starting to show that something very significant was happening and that the former ways of understanding and living a religious life were being completely changed:

> Truly I tell you, among those born of women there has not risen anyone greater than John the Baptist; yet whoever is least in the kingdom of heaven is greater than he. From the days of John the Baptist until now, the kingdom of heaven has been subjected to violence, and violent people have been raiding it. For all the Prophets and the Law prophesied until John. And if you are willing to

accept it, he is the Elijah who was to come. Whoever has ears, let them hear.
(Matthew 11:11-15)

He specifically refers to John the Baptist as Elijah,[9] making a clear link back to the very end of the last book of the Old Testament, bridging the silent gap of 400 years since God last spoke to Israel and powerfully opening a new chapter in what it means to know and follow God.

Jesus says that 'there has not risen anyone greater than John the Baptist' (v11). He is the zenith standing at the head of the long and illustrious tradition of the prophets and so could be thought of as the greatest; not only is he the last example of this tradition, but he is also the one who passes the baton to the One towards whom the whole story has been working. He is the one who pulls the curtain aside to reveal Jesus and inaugurates Him into His public ministry. He actually baptises the Messiah; nothing or no one could be more significant than that! This is the culmination, the completion and fulfilment of the Law and Prophets as Jesus the Christ finally accomplishes all that is set out for Him to do.[10] It is tragically fitting that the best and the last of the soon to be superseded old covenant tradition should end his days like this in prison.

Jesus begins to say that the old way is being wound up and that it is being brought to a timely conclusion, not because it has been a failure, but because it has done what it was meant to do. The Law and the Prophets were looking forward to something that has now finally arrived

---

[9] See the prophecy in Malachi 4:5-6.
[10] Matthew 5:17.

and so they are being set aside as having fulfilled their purpose. Paul argues this at some length in Galatians,[11] which we will look at in chapter 7. From now on, even the most seemingly insignificant person who accepts God's kingdom and lives by it, hearing Jesus and following Him, is greater, simply because they are living in a time of fulfilment.

Jesus knew the Father as no one else did. It must have been hard for Him as those around him, disciples included, did not have the same depth of awareness of the Father as He did. Picking up on the comment about '[playing] the pipe for you, and you did not dance' (v17), let me use the image or metaphor of music for a moment.

Only Jesus knew the song of creation; He knew the tune to which creation was called to dance. He knew the songs the stars sing and He knew what it was to sing in tune with this eternal song as He wrote it in the first place, being the unique composer and conductor of this ceaseless melody. Everyone thought they knew the song and believed they were singing in tune, as their song was, of course, the correct version but, in reality, there was a jarring variation between the different groups and their disparate songs. The Pharisees sang one tune and the Sadducees another, and so on. The disharmony for the One who had 'perfect pitch' and the misrepresentation of His beloved Father must have been dreadful.

These strident disharmonies could be said by comparison to make the song that Jesus sang, and calls us all to sing, much sweeter and clearer. They thought that the song of educational training, years of intellectual

---

[11] Galatians 3–4.

scholarship, endless discussion and theories regarding weighty and complicated matters – perhaps a bit like some religious leaders today – was the song that needed to be sung, and how they liked the sound of their own voices!

Jesus cuts right through this and calls us to sing a different tune, the original tune that even a child can hear and understand, along with tax collectors and sinners, who in many cases can better appreciate the beauty of this song.

Jesus goes on to denounce that generation in the strongest possible terms and is stinging in His rebuke of them, calling out their arrogant shortsightedness by saying that they have criticised John the Baptist for doing one thing and yet accused the Son of Man for doing the opposite. The tragedy of the moment is immense and palpable.

It hadn't worked: Matthew 11:20-24

A discussion ensues about the nearby towns of Chorazin and Bethsaida being compared to Tyre and Sidon, and Capernaum to Sodom. Tyre, Sidon and Sodom were notorious for their wickedness. For all the miracles done, all the prophets prophesying, all the tireless poring over the law, all the endless debates about what such and such a law meant and how it should be applied to current situations, all the additional laws that had been created to ringfence and protect the original 613 Mosaic laws,[12] it

---

[12] The thinking followed that if breaking the Law of Moses, which comprised 613 statutes, caused the devastating results of exile, then it made sense to have further laws, like an outer fence protecting the

clearly had not worked. This would have been self-evident to anyone with eyes to see or ears to hear, as Jesus often said, to what was going on in Jerusalem at the time. Israel was not the nation it had been called to be, certainly not doing the things it was meant to do and definitely not being that light to the nations.[13] Israel was not living up – by any stretch of the imagination – to being that blessed people and, in turn, being a blessing to the world, as originally promised by God to Abram in Genesis 12:2-3, when he was called to follow Him.

In condemning Chorazin, Bethsaida and Capernaum, Jesus pointed out that even Tyre, Sidon and Sodom would have grasped what was being said and done, but yet these places in Israel had not. There are many other examples in Jesus' short three years when He highlighted that things were not as they should be. The temple worship for one, the endless law-giving which, far from freeing people, had done the exact opposite. Yes, one thing was clear: it had not worked!

God was finally calling time on this old system.

Childlike relationship: Matthew 11:25-27

Jesus now changes the whole tone of the discourse, turns things and their understanding right around by referring to 'little children' (v25). This would have been a comedown for the intellectual and self-righteous leaders. The religious and so-called learned among the crowd would not have appreciated this, but the ordinary people

---

inner fence of the original 613. Ezra and others were thought of as writing and implementing these additional protective laws.
[13] Isaiah 42:6, NASB.

would have got it immediately and enjoyed it immensely. Not only in seeing the pious religious among them taken down a peg or two but, more crucially, although they may not have been able to put a finger on it, they were for the first time breathing the fresh oxygen of grace into their lives and their faith.

Jesus is heralding a completely different way of understanding God in contrasting the intellectual arrogance of the learned with the purity of childlike faith. This paradigm shift challenges the pharisaic reliance on law and knowledge, replacing it with relationship and grace. It is a fresh breath of childlike innocence contrasting against a cynical, weary, worn-out way of continual striving. The tree of the knowledge of good and evil did not bring the benefits promised by the snake in the garden. Israel drank deeply from this tree as they expounded on the law, using knowledge of good and evil, to address and solve the very problems caused by it in the first place![14] Jesus calls us all back to an innocence of relationship, of life rather than knowledge and intellectual expertise. Not a naivete, as we have all been wounded by sin, but a freedom of innocence of a loving, grace-filled relationship rather than a crippling awareness of guilt caused by the law.

After denouncing the generation of that time as the culmination and ripe example of the inability of the old way of doing things to bring change and life, Jesus brings a radically new way. He begins to lay out His unique credentials to bring that much-needed fresh

---

[14] Rick Joyner, *There Were Two Trees in The Garden*, New Kensington, PA: Whitaker House, 1993.

understanding and insight to the whole mess. In effect He is saying, 'Up to now your way of thinking has been wrong. You have looked at the Law and the Prophets, interpreting them as though looking through the wrong end of a telescope [I know they didn't have telescopes then!], having the wrong perspective and making it so small.' They have misunderstood the whole broad intent of God, reducing it to something small, controlling and self-centred.

Jesus has a unique Father–Son relationship and thus has an accurate and faithful perspective; He is looking at this as One who was there at creation, when life was breathed into humankind, when the laws were given and so also as the One who understands the intention behind them. Jesus makes an astonishing claim that only He knows the Father and that the Father knows Him, that thus He alone can know and understand the reasoning, the thinking and the plan behind it all:

> All things have been committed to me by my Father. No one knows the Son except the Father, and no one knows the Father except the Son and those to whom the Son chooses to reveal him.
> (Matthew 11:27)

This verse is a crucial lens not only through which to view the following verses, but also to understanding much of the New Testament revelation of the work of Christ. Jesus refers to Himself frequently, often in connection to His revelations about the nature of God and Himself, as the Son. This is a huge subject and much too big to be covered here, but as an indication of what is being touched upon are Jesus' own words, 'if the Son sets you free, you will be free indeed,'[15] where His liberating message is couched in terms of His Sonship to the Father. We will return to this in subsequent chapters.

We gain a deep insight as we see Jesus, in this personal prayer, giving thanks and revealing that His deepest calling and motivation is obedience to the Father. We see this play out throughout His life and death. Our Trinitarian faith in God is that the Christ as revealed in Jesus is an integral and equal part of the Trinity and so must, of course, be obedient to the Father, but also to His own true nature as the Christ. He could not be any other, and here we see the reality of this relationship playing out in that the Son is utterly trustworthy and wholly obedient to the Father, which means that all things can be, and are, committed to Him. The Son is not a hierarchical or even chronological place but an authoritative position from which Jesus can say, 'Anyone who has seen me has seen the Father' (John 14:9).

Jesus draws a very strong parallel by comparing how little children are the ones who will come to know His Father, and in this same breath saying how this reflects His relationship with His Father. His relationship with God the Father reveals and is even the original intended model for our relationship with God. In this short verse, Jesus gives the basis for realigning humankind's understanding of God and the whole nature of religion. It's based on relationship, not religious observance.

---

[15] John 8:36.

Sabbath: Matthew 12:1-14

After the section in verses 28 to 30, which we will come back to in a moment, Matthew continues straight into discussing the Sabbath. Chapters in our Bibles were added around 700 years ago, so a break has been inserted in the narrative that was not there originally. We know that Sabbath observance was a fundamental aspect of the Mosaic Law; however, Jesus challenged the rigid and legalistic interpretations that had come to dominate its practice. Matthew highlights this at some length in chapter 12, as do all the Gospel writers. Sabbath was one of the core definitions of what it meant to be a Jew, along with a few others, including food laws and circumcision. By highlighting Sabbath observance, Matthew brings into sharp focus the confused thinking and contradictions of the law and those who sought to apply it.

After being questioned about plucking corn on the Sabbath, Jesus talks about David and even the priests in the temple, desecrating the Sabbath to serve God. He then makes a pivotal statement:

> I tell you that something greater than the temple is here. If you had known what these words mean, 'I desire mercy, not sacrifice,' you would not have condemned the innocent. For the Son of Man is Lord of the Sabbath.
> (Matthew 12:6-8)

A remarkable claim is made that Jesus is greater than the temple, which by default would include the whole Mosaic Law system, including the Sabbath. Directly after this, Jesus audaciously goes on to make a point of healing a man with a shrivelled hand, and in doing so again highlights the contradictions in their thinking about Sabbath keeping.

In saying that 'something greater than the temple is here', Jesus gives notice that the temple era and all the rules and regulations surrounding it have come to an end. This includes the traditional view and interpretation of the Sabbath.

Sabbath laws had evolved into a complicated web of restrictions that transformed a day of rest into a burdensome observance. The simple commandment forbidding work was further defined with thirty-nine basic actions, among which were reaping, winnowing, threshing and preparing a meal. But not just that; for instance, they had to define what a burden was, concluding that it was anything that weighed as much as two dried figs. In the Book of Jubilees 50:8 it says, 'And the man that does any work on it shall die: whoever desecrates that day, whoever lies with (his) wife, or whoever says he will do something on it, that he will set out on a journey thereon in regard to any buying or selling.'[16] Even the contemplation of work was not allowed.

When we look back to Jesus' comments about John the Baptist in Matthew 11:11-15, we see that what He was laying out then has now come into sharp focus. The

---

[16] www.yahwehswordarchives.org/book_of_jubilees/book_of_jubilees_chapter_50.htm (accessed 3rd April 2025). Book of Jubilees is a book found in the Apocrypha, which comprises Jewish writings between the Old and New Testament times. Some branches of the Christian Church consider these not to be authoritative while others put more weight on them. Whatever your view, they are at least an indication of thinking at that time.

temple, Sabbath and, as we read later in Matthew 12, even the food laws are now to be entirely reframed. Reframed not in a strange way, ripping them completely out of context, but placing them firmly back into God's original intention.

In the Old Testament, the highest revelation of truth was the Ten Commandments, which were inanimate decrees carved on stone, whereas in the New Testament, the highest revelation of truth is a relationship with Jesus Christ. Jesus said, 'I am the way and the truth and the life' (John 14:6). Being in a living relationship with the Truth is what sets you free. When Jesus makes His invitation to come to Him, it is addressed to those on whom the Pharisees have laid heavy burdens by demanding meticulous, crushing obedience, not only to the law but also to their own elaborate interpretations of the law.

An invitation: Matthew 11:28-30

Now that Jesus has laid out His credentials for those who have ears to hear, He makes His invitation to 'come to Me': come into that living and life-giving relationship. He calls us all to a relationship with the One who creates and sustains all things, for whom all things were created,[17] and who understands to the very core of His being what this is really all about. In the centre of this radical reframing of all that the religious-minded of the day held dear, Jesus breathes that wonderful oxygen of grace with His glorious words, 'Come to me.' It reflects God breathing life into Adam at creation, and here Jesus is breathing life back into the lifeless corpse of religion.

---

[17] Colossians 1:16.

Jesus talks about being weary and burdened and finding rest, which reflects that wonderful passage in Isaiah:

> Come, all you who are thirsty,
> come to the waters;
> and you who have no money,
> come, buy and eat!
> Come, buy wine and milk
> without money and without cost.
> Why spend money on what is not bread,
> and your labour on what does not satisfy?
> Listen, listen to me, and eat what is good,
> and you will delight in the richest of fare.
> (Isaiah 55:1-2)

This chapter in Isaiah finishes with:

> You will go out in joy
> and be led forth in peace;
> the mountains and hills
> will burst into song before you,
> and all the trees of the field
> will clap their hands.
> Instead of the thorn-bush will grow the juniper,
> and instead of briers the myrtle will grow.
> (Isaiah 55:12-13)

As mentioned earlier, I love how Eugene Petersen in *The Message* phrases our key passage in Matthew. It bears repeating here:

> Are you tired? Worn out? Burned out on religion?
> Come to me. Get away with me and you'll recover

> your life. I'll show you how to take a real rest. Walk with me and work with me – watch how I do it. Learn the unforced rhythms of grace. I won't lay anything heavy or ill-fitting on you. Keep company with me and you'll learn to live freely and lightly. (Matthew 11:28-30, *The Message*)

As one who has been a Christian for most of my life, and also as a former pastor, this rings true, and I think for many who do not follow Christ but have observed many Christians, this will be recognisable. They often observe a faith that talks of freedom and forgiveness and yet its followers seem to be living the opposite, and so they choose to reject these life-giving and affirming words of invitation.

In the next chapters, I want to take this wonderful passage and breathe some fresh air into our understanding of rest, unpacking it in hopefully a fresh and life-giving way. Over the years, oxygen has been sucked out of the life-giving promises of God until they have become suffocating. Grace breathes oxygen back into what it means to be known by God. Many may think and believe that they know God through their own intellect, but it is Jesus who not only reveals and makes God known as Father, but can also bring us into that unique Father–child relationship. No other faith or religion promises that or even comes close. Jesus stands out as uniquely supreme in this claim.

To the pastors among us, Ajith Fernando calls for rest and peace in a hurried and pressured world.[18] With our

---

[18] Ajith Fernando, *Jesus Driven Ministry*, Leicester: IVP, 2002, p 63.

congregations so often facing pressures from many directions, the pastor cannot lead them into peace-bringing rest if they themselves are stressed. That, of course, does not equate to being idle and lazy, but it does call for a different way of walking and leading. Fernando comments that over-activity is one of the great pitfalls for a pastor. God calls us to repent and rest, to be still and in our stillness to know God,[19] and this is as important now as it was then. Some pastors and church members may question this as they are so invested in performance-based church activity that to admit anything else is beyond thought. I know from personal experience that pastors can feel a very real pressure of having to 'keep the show on the road', carrying the weight of responsibility for the church members and knowing the guilt of not performing as expected, while the church members who are themselves working hard and giving sacrificially certainly do not want to see their pastor taking it easy on the back of their hard work! This means that Jesus' words are every bit as important now as they were then.

Summary

We have seen that Jesus' teaching in Matthew 11–12 specifically addresses the proven inadequacy of the former way of faith, making it clear that a new beginning is not only needed but has now come. This new beginning is embodied in Jesus and is founded on the basis of His relationship with His Father, which is the very foundation of creation itself. This relationship not only brings the fresh wind of a new start but also, uniquely, has the

---

[19] Isaiah 30:15; Psalm 46:10.

qualifications to do so. We need to dig further to find a way through and breathe this oxygen for all of us!

Waymarker

Sit
Find a quiet still place where you can review what we have looked at in this chapter, and allow your feelings to bubble up.

Commit this time to the Lord as you ask Him to speak to you and bring anything to mind or heart which He wants to show you.

Reflect
What emotions or feelings do the words of Jesus inviting us to come to Him to rest evoke in your heart? You don't have to put words to these feelings or even understand them; just acknowledging them is enough.

Which tune have you been dancing to? Has it always been this way?

Pray
Bring these emotions, thoughts and impressions to God as an offering, placing them into the safety of His hands. Commit to Him the journey He is taking you on, leaving it open-ended and trusting Him to lead you.

4
A traditional understanding

> The best way to get a bad law repealed is to enforce it strictly.
> *Abraham Lincoln*[20]

Having looked at the context of Jesus' words in Matthew, we now turn to consider the traditional understanding and cultural background of a yoke and labouring. We like to keep things safe and in line with our existing understanding so we are not challenged, keeping us comfortable. If we want to think differently and follow Jesus' teaching, we must be able to look at what the traditional thinking was then and how it applies today.

A yoke

We are all familiar with the most common idea of a yoke as harnessing one or more animals by placing a wooden bar across their shoulders so that implements can be pulled or burdens carried. Accordingly, it is usually associated with work and effort in carrying or pulling a load of some kind, but the word can also refer to:

---

[20] www.goodreads.com/quotes/508834-the-best-way-to-get-a-bad-law-repealed-is (accessed 3rd April 2025).

- a measurement of how many oxen you had.[21] We use this idea today when we talk about a brace of pheasants as meaning two;
- a set of scales contrasting one comparable thing against another, be it effort, weight, mass or even volume;
- an integral part of clothing where a yoke is the piece of material which is around the neck from which the rest of the garment hangs and is secured in place;
- the control which a plane's pilot holds to steer and operate the aircraft.

The word 'yoke', as both a noun and a verb, originates from an old European term meaning to join or fasten. Figuratively, it came to symbolise 'burden' or 'servitude' in old English. Whatever the context, it is always used in relation to joining. Unsurprisingly, it follows that we usually think of a yoke, or being yoked, in terms of work and effort. We automatically carry this idea over to our faith as well, which in many ways strikes me as a contradiction. I think Paul did too, as he says in Ephesians 2:8 that it is not by our effort or work that we are saved, but by God's gift of grace. However, it is a natural step to automatically apply this idea of work to what Jesus is saying in Matthew 11.

Burdensome work

We assume that when yoked or joined to another, we should share the load equally, be it carrying or pulling

---

[21] 1 Kings 19:19.

something. If two oxen are yoked, I would think that they must both pull approximately equally or things will go badly wrong. The furrow would surely be crooked with one animal not really pulling its weight while the other works harder to compensate; so, as well as bad ploughing, I presume it would be uncomfortable for both. Some may think of a stronger animal being yoked with a weaker one so that the stronger one complements and makes up for and at the same time trains the weaker one. Either way, the weaker animal must work harder or the stronger one work less so as not to put a strain on the other's shoulders. The yoke is placed equally across both animals' shoulders, so if one pulls harder then it must be very uncomfortable for the other animal, as the yoke will no longer sit easily as it is dragged along by the neck.

When we take this analogy, which we usually do, as being yoked with Jesus in this way, it means we must either work harder, taking an equal weight, or expect Jesus as the stronger partner to hold back! This is arrogant in the extreme, making us equal with Jesus in what we do, and in turn places a weight of expectation on us which is impossible to bear. Alternatively, the idea that Jesus, in His grace, is holding back in carrying us, that He is pulling us along as well as whatever is behind, can create a sense of worthlessness which is also difficult to bear.

I subscribed to that view for many years and thought how wonderful it was to be yoked with Jesus, to work with Him in his harvest. But I found that placed an impossible burden of expectation on me which I could never live up to and caused a deep sense of failure. To state the obvious: I am not Jesus and I am not Jesus' equal.

Performance-based religion

There are many references to co-working in the New Testament. For instance, 1 Corinthians 3:9 says that we are 'fellow workers' with each other in God's work. It is not that we are co-workers with God, but as Paul was with Apollos, likewise we are in God's field; here we read that the Corinthians are like a field or a building, which Paul then expands on. We also find elsewhere:

> I entreat Eu-o'dia and I entreat Syn'tyche to agree in the Lord. And I ask you also, true yokefellow, help these women, for they have labored side by side with me in the gospel together with Clement and the rest of my fellow workers, whose names are in the book of life.
> (Philippians 4:2-3, RSV)

This phrase clearly refers to the people of God working together in God's field, working and serving, and not in relation to being yoked with Jesus. In John's Gospel we are told what the works of God are – and please note that nowhere does it include labouring:

> Believe me when I say that I am in the Father and the Father is in me; or at least believe on the evidence of the works themselves. Very truly I tell you, whoever believes in me will do the works I have been doing, and they will do even greater things than these, because I am going to the Father.
> (John 14:11-12)

Jesus also says elsewhere that the work He wants us to do is to believe in Him.[22] It is very clear that the work God requires is for us to believe. James reminds us that this belief should turn to action, saying that if it doesn't then it is not faith at all.[23] So I am most certainly not arguing for inactive faith.

Paul seems to give a very simple test to see if people are in the faith or not. He calls us to look at ourselves honestly to see if we truly believe that Christ is in us, in 2 Corinthians 13:5. The test for authentic faith is simple: do we acknowledge that Jesus Christ is really in us? The apostle John in his letters says clearly that the only thing which is important, even crucial, to salvation, is to believe that Jesus Christ came 'in the flesh', that 'Jesus is the Son of God' and 'is the Christ'; it's that simple (1 John 4:2,15; 5:1) Why do we complicate it so? Nowhere does our salvation depend on how hard we work, yet in many circles this seems to be the case!

We can be so caught up in this idea of performance-based faith that we are driven, fearful of being found wanting by either God or people. I have heard this performance-based idea of faith preached many times as a surefire method of making people feel inadequate and guilty. The insinuation that is often used is that somehow we are lacking, based on Daniel 5:25-27, that we are being weighed and come up short. This goes back to one of the ideas that a yoke is like a set of scales. It is so easy to use this technique to make people more susceptible to feeling guilty. However, when we look at this phrase in context,

---

[22] John 6:28-29.
[23] James 2:17.

we see that it refers to Belshazzar, king of the Babylonians, and not to Christ's followers, so using it in the context of how hard we work is to take it completely out of place.

In Matthew we read of Jesus speaking of the Pharisees: 'They tie up heavy, cumbersome loads and put them on other people's shoulders, but they themselves are not willing to lift a finger to move them' (Matthew 23:4). The understanding of that day which Jesus refers to and denounces is that the religious leaders liked to tell the people that they were inadequate and found wanting. This was exactly what was happening, and again reinforces the thinking that faith is about works and in turn tells us that Jesus is coming from a different perspective.

Robbed of joy

Many of us have felt the pressure that robs the joy from serving in church. The pressure of rotas we must be part of, projects we must support and meetings we must attend, etc. The need to carry our weight and play our part quickly becomes a measure of our commitment to the church and of our faith in God. Of course, we must serve and play our part in any family, but when it is out of a sense of guilt, we are only perpetuating the old way.

The yoke was a symbol of servitude in the Bible. To emphasise the weight of oppression, the yoke is sometimes described as 'iron',[24] and was a metaphor for the burden of slavery or taxes upon the people.[25] Freedom

---

[24] Deuteronomy 28:48.
[25] 1 Kings 12:10-11.

from oppression was described in poetic and prophetic literature as breaking the yoke.[26]

Jeremiah was commanded to go about Jerusalem wearing a wooden yoke on his neck, and to send a message to the kings of the neighbouring countries, that they too would be subject to Babylonian rule.[27] In a dramatic public confrontation with Hananiah, who was a false prophet, he broke the yoke which Jeremiah was wearing as a sign that Israel would be released from Babylon. In response, Jeremiah prophesied correctly that in place of the yoke of wood, there would come a 'yoke of iron' (Jeremiah 28:10-17). Using the idea of a yoke of iron takes the hardness and unforgiving nature to an extreme length and takes the idea of wearing to its inevitable conclusion, which we see unfolding through history. A wooden yoke is bad enough, no matter how well fitting, but a cold lump of iron is unbearable.

Mishnah and Torah

To further our understanding of the times in which our passage in Matthew was spoken, we can look at how it was reflected in the Mishnah. The Mishnah was the collection of rabbinic traditions that helped in understanding and applying the Torah, the Mosaic Law. For example, the command 'Remember the Sabbath day' and 'Observe the Sabbath day' (Exodus 20:8-11; Deuteronomy 5:12-15 respectively), is unpacked. The Mishnah is unique within the rabbinic tradition and plays a key role in the religious

---

[26] See Isaiah 10:27.
[27] Jeremiah 27:2-6, Jeremiah 28:14.

life of the Jewish people.[28] It is appropriate to take a moment to look at this, as Matthew's Gospel was primarily written to a Jewish audience whose understanding of faith would inevitably been greatly influenced by the thinking at that time.[29]

In rabbinic understanding, the idea of the yoke was important and could be seen as the symbol of service and servitude. For the Jew, the principle that they should be freed from servitude to people to devote themselves to the service of God was significant, with the 'yoke of the kingdom of man' being contrasted with 'the yoke of the kingdom of heaven'. Rabbi Nechunia son of Hakanah said:

> Whoever takes upon himself the yoke of the Torah, they remove from him the yoke of government and the yoke of worldly concerns, and whoever breaks off from himself the yoke of the Torah, they place upon him the yoke of government and the yoke of worldly concerns
> (Pirkei Avot 3:5)[30]

As I write, the war between Israel and Hamas in Gaza is raging, and there is discussion in the Israeli parliament about whether orthodox Jews should serve in the army.

---

[28] www.jewishvirtuallibrary.org/mishnah (accessed 10th August 2024).
[29] The Mishnah was first published as a document in the second century AD, recording oral tradition. Although it was not in existence at the time of Jesus, it reflects the thinking of that time. www.myjewishlearning.com/article/mishnah (accessed 7th April 2025).
[30] www.sefaria.org/English_Explanation_of_Pirkei_Avot.3.5.2?lang=bi (accessed 12th March 2025).

The Orthodox Jews argue that they are exempt from civil duties because they are studying the Torah.

The 'yoke of the Torah' therefore refers to the duty of devoting oneself to study. Proclamation of the unity of God by reading the Shema[31] is called 'accepting upon oneself the yoke of the kingdom of heaven', while the acceptance of the fulfilment of the commandments as a whole is referred to in the second paragraph of the Shema and is called 'accepting the yoke of the Commandments'.

In quoting from Pirkei Avot 6:6, we can gain insight into the requirements of accepting the yoke of the Torah. The passage outlines forty-eight attributes necessary for attaining the Torah and becoming a true disciple. Each requirement builds upon the previous one – for example, it begins with the necessity of study, which is made possible through attentive listening. Attentive listening, in turn, depends on proper speech, which stems from having an understanding heart. This progression continues through another forty-two attributes, finishing with the disciple's responsibility to be precise in their learning and to accurately say a thing in the name of the teacher who said it.[32]

The last line of Pirkei Avot 6:6 (see footnote 32), in particular, and the drift of the whole passage can be seen as a reference to the idea of the rabbi's yoke. It is an impossible goal for anyone to attain and an enormous burden, probably causing a crushing sense of failure. Maybe that was the unspoken intention? In some ways

---

[31] Shema, the Jewish confession of faith made up of three scriptural texts: Deuteronomy 6:4-9; 11:13-21; Numbers 15:37-41

[32] www.sefaria.org/Pirkei_Avot.6?lang=en (accessed 12th March 2025).

this is similar to the list which Peter gives in 2 Peter 1:5-7, where he encourages the ongoing addition of one quality to another. However, Peter's much shorter list of eight attributes is gracious and ends with love.

We can see how easy it would have been for the Pharisees to make people feel inadequate; what with these requirements as well as all the other laws, it truly was a burden that was crushing. It is in this cultural context that Jesus goes on to talk about heavy burdens and rest. He mentions rest twice and also learning, not in the context of wisdom or understanding, but in relationship.

To learn the Torah was a full-time occupation to which only the best and those who had the ability and dedication were called. Years of devoted study to the exclusion of much else meant it was for the elite, who of course liked to consider themselves better than the others, and they certainly encouraged everyone else to see them that way! The process by which a young Jewish boy was educated and considered to be the disciple of a rabbi was strenuous. From the age of six to ten, he would attend a synagogue school five days a week, where he would be taught the Torah, and by the end of those years would be expected to know those books off by heart. From the age of ten to fourteen years, the boy would attend another school where he would memorise the rest of the Scriptures and learn the Jewish art of answering a question by a question. We know that Jesus was already good at this by the time he was twelve, as we read that when He was left behind in Jerusalem and His parents found Him in the temple, He was asking questions![33]

---

[33] Luke 2:46.

The rabbi's yoke

Then, when a boy turned thirteen or fourteen and had done well, he would approach a rabbi and ask if he could follow him, with the rabbi testing him to see if he was good enough; he only wanted disciples who could learn and continue his teaching. This was known as the rabbi's yoke. If the rabbi was satisfied that a boy was up to it, he would say, 'Come, take my yoke and follow me and be my disciple.' The boy would then go with the rabbi wherever he travelled and devote his entire life to learn from the rabbi, his yoke, his interpretation of the Scriptures. If the boy was not up to it, he would be told to go back to his family and learn a trade. Consequently, the yoke of the Torah was out of reach for the majority of people and, of course, definitely children, and little children at that! When Jesus calls the children, He is speaking directly into this thinking.

Thus, the word 'yoke' in this context can be understood to describe the teaching of a rabbi.[34] As we have seen, the Torah is very complex in the way it needs to be applied to all sorts of different situations in daily life. For instance, walking a certain distance on the Sabbath in the eyes of one rabbi is permitted, while another says you can walk twice that far, or another would say you can only walk half that distance without breaking the Sabbath rest.

Another example would be the discussion around divorce. The law in Deuteronomy 24:1-4 was applied in different ways by different rabbis. Rabbi Shammai and his

---

[34] Rob Bell, *Velvet Elvis: Repainting the Christian Faith*, Grand Rapids, MI: Zondervan, 2005, pp40f. This book introduced me to the idea of the rabbi's yoke, which led to me further research and conversations.

school taught that the legitimate grounds for divorce was adultery, that was his yoke, while Rabbi Hillel taught that anything that displeased a husband – such as being belligerent or burning the bread – would be good enough.

Rabbis taught their yoke to their disciples, their interpretation of the Torah. The yoke was not primarily about the rabbi, but how the rabbi applied and understood the Torah. So we see that the rabbi's yoke was the interpretation of the Torah and the keeping of the Torah. We can see elsewhere in Scripture that the term 'yoke of the law' was in common usage. We read in Acts:

> Now then, why do you try to test God by putting on the necks of Gentiles a yoke that neither we nor our ancestors have been able to bear? No! We believe it is through the grace of our Lord Jesus that we are saved, just as they are.
> (Acts 15:10-11)

Peter voiced what they all knew and what Jesus addressed in Matthew 11: that the yoke of the law was unbearable. I wonder if Peter and the others had felt like second-rate Jews, as in their youth they had not 'made the grade' and so were emotionally involved in this?

Jesus speaks

Jesus called His disciples to accept His yoke, His interpretation of the law, but how different this understanding was. This was not an obedience to any external law, but a relationship to a person, which enables a completely different kind of loyalty and joy in following. Jesus said in John 14:15 that if people loved Him, they would keep His commands, as a loving relationship always makes the burden, or yoke, easier. 'Learn from me,' he said, 'for I am gentle and humble in heart' (Matthew 11:29), which is a very different concept of God.

It is interesting to note that Jesus did not say, 'I will teach you,' but instead said, 'Learn from me.' Teaching and learning are obviously intertwined, but there is a difference in that teaching is imparting information with an emphasis on intellectual knowledge, while learning is about receiving and, crucially, putting into practice. Jesus was saying that He will enable us to learn and live practically His new way of living. It is not an intellectual exercise, but a way of living that all can enter into. I wonder if Jesus talked about it this way to differentiate His way of learning and discipleship from the established ways of that time.

Jesus came to wipe the slate clean and bring a different understanding from the one that had grown over the centuries. It had become impossible to keep and had changed into an intolerable burden rather than the life-affirming gift it had originally been. This yoke, be it the application of Torah, rabbinic teaching or, today, straining to do our best, pulling our weight, trying to keep up, had not and does not and never will work in producing the works and fruits of righteousness.

The rest Jesus refers to is a rest from work, not an increase. We must reconsider exactly what the yoke that Jesus refers to is and what this rest really looks like.

Summary

A yoke can be seen as the rabbi's or teacher's interpretation and application of the Torah. The rabbi calls the best to be his disciples, which would be male adults of some financial means. Jesus cut right across this, making this accessible to all: to women, tax collectors, sinners, the poor and even children, all of whom would not even be able to make the first cut of traditional rabbinic teaching. No wonder people responded in the way they did to Jesus.

Waymarker

Sit
Find a comfortable place where you can be at peace without interruption.

Reflect
Some thoughts to ponder.

A well-fitting, rigid yoke leaves no room for growth. Is there an aspect of your faith that was valuable at one time, but you have now outgrown?

Can the law actually grow us spiritually, or does it confine us to a 'robotic' faith?

In your life of faith, what or who are you following? A living Saviour or a doctrine-based code of practice?

Pray
Bring your thoughts and feelings to God and ask Him to teach and lead you in to the truth of your relationship with Him, as that is what will set you free.

5
The gift

> We cannot solve our problems with the same thinking we used when we created them.
> *Albert Einstein*[35]

A new thing

Jesus, as we have seen, brought a fresh understanding of the law and promise of God. It was new but not novel. Like so much of God's revelation, it is new to us, but when we trace it back, we see that it certainly is not novel, but deeply rooted in history. I have seen that in my own life as God has led me into new things, but when I look back, I find I can see His hand moving all along!

When we consider snowflakes and how each one is different, we glimpse the continuing infinite creativity of God. We should not be surprised when God says that He does a new thing:

> See, I am doing a new thing!
> Now it springs up; do you not perceive it?
> I am making a way in the wilderness
> and streams in the wasteland.
> (Isaiah 43:19)

---

[35] www.brainyquote.com/quotes/albert_einstein_121993 (accessed 4th April 2025).

Scripture should always challenge us, but we prefer to interpret it according to our tried, tested and comfortable ways. In doing this it can lose its cutting edge in our lives. While humanity is very creative, for good and bad, in reality we only apply and use what is already in existence. God, when He says He does a new thing, means exactly that!

We need to let the Holy Spirit use Scripture to continually open our eyes to fresh revelations of grace, as the 'new thing' God speaks of will definitely not align with our current understanding, otherwise it simply wouldn't be new! Revelation is not to the learned or astute as it works on an entirely different principle, for instance to little children; that's why it's called revelation rather than education. Jesus pointedly talks about those 'little ones' who do not know and have not even had an opportunity to memorise the Torah (Matthew 10:42). The expectations of our current thinking are not even applicable to little children, and as such, our understanding must be based on something quite different.

There are many ways to grasp this, and, for example, we find these important words in Paul's letter to the Romans:

> Nevertheless, death reigned from the time of Adam to the time of Moses, even over those who did not sin by breaking a command, as did Adam, who is a pattern of the one to come.
> But the gift is not like the trespass. For if the many died by the trespass of the one man, how much more did God's grace and the gift that came by the grace of the one man, Jesus Christ, overflow to

> the many! Nor can the gift of God be compared with the result of one man's sin: the judgment followed one sin and brought condemnation, but the gift followed many trespasses and brought justification.
> (Romans 5:14-16)

Paul, the most learned of the apostles, who could rely on his education and sharp intellect more than anyone, knew that a new way of understanding was needed. In this passage we see two key things which are often overlooked: 'the gift is not like the trespass', and 'the gift of God [cannot] be compared'. In other words, the grace provided is not like the sin forgiven, and the life given is not like the death overcome.

Paul takes this to heart, building his life on it, as we can see by the passage in Philippians 3:4-10, particularly verse 8:

> What is more, I consider everything a loss because of the surpassing worth of knowing Christ Jesus my Lord, for whose sake I have lost all things. I consider them garbage, that I may gain Christ.
> (Philippians 3:8)

Salvation and the gift of grace are *not* like a set of scales. With scales we compare like for like, be it weight, mass or distance; irrespective of units used, it is still the same thing on both sides, it is still like for like.

Balancing scales

We often think of the work of Jesus as being like a set of scales comparing His grace against our sin, His work of redemption against our slavery, His love against the world's hate. Happily, we know that the scales always come down in Jesus' favour! Then we make it personal: His achievement outweighs our failure, His beauty outweighs our ugliness, His sacrifice outweighs our sin and as we know, of course, His power always outweighs Satan's. We could go on making these comparisons. These are all certainly true and a blessing, but we fall short, making a fundamental error in considering the gift to be like the trespass, in that we measure and compare one against the other.

Jesus in His teaching brings a fresh view, that 'new thing', which Paul takes, clearly saying in his own words that 'the gift is not like the trespass'; they are completely different and cannot be compared!

When a comparison is made, the enemy and his works are elevated to a status to which they do not and cannot have as created beings, while the love, grace and power of God is devalued to such an extent that it is no longer the unique work of the creator God. By comparing, we reduce God to the status of the created and only slightly above the rest. That to me is an appalling thought. No, the two are incomparable! How can you compare the Creator with the creation? It's as absurd as trying to put a weight on one side of a set of scales and something completely different, like love, on the other. They are so different that they cannot be compared. It's ludicrous, but it is what we do.

Maybe the idea of measuring and comparing in such a manner was appropriate to the old way before Jesus, but He firmly says that is now fulfilled and we don't have to, nor should we, think like that any more. The new has come and the old has gone! This is taken and further applied in 2 Corinthians:

> So from now on we regard no one from a worldly point of view. Though we once regarded Christ in this way, we do so no longer. Therefore, if anyone is in Christ, the new creation has come: the old has gone, the new is here!
> (2 Corinthians 5:16-17)

There is an emphatic 'don't do that' in this passage: don't compare the old with the new creation and don't compare ourselves or others. We struggle with that as many live in a world of scarcity, needing always to measure, because we feel that there is never enough to go around. This affects how we think about ourselves, viewing others as competition. It certainly applies when we want to buy something as basic as petrol to put in our car, or energy to heat our homes. We measure when resources are limited or costs need to be covered

When there is a limitless, infinite supply, measurement becomes meaningless. Infinity can be defined as something limitless, boundless or greater than any quantity or number. You simply can't measure it! Thankfully, however, with God who is infinite, there is infinite grace, which we cannot measure and it's pointless to try to measure, as it is beyond measuring! We never need to worry whether God's grace is enough to cover our sin; indeed we are told that He not only forgives but also forgets.[36]

---

[36] Isaiah 43:25; Psalm 103:12.

Then we can go even further, thinking and saying of ourselves or others that I or they just don't measure up. Measuring with that attitude belongs firmly to the Mosaic Law which Jesus, of course, completed and fulfilled.[37] So often we can be our own worst critics, beating ourselves up time and time again for things we have or have not done. That can be a brutal yoke, but in the gift of grace, Jesus frees us from that. When we consider and factor in Satan, the accuser, who is so busy, proficient and practised at accusing, we may end up with an unbearable and life-sapping yoke. This can drive many to a feeling of total failure and despair that they simply can't go on, and so they give up.

'But the gift is not like the trespass'; we have been set free from this.

God calls us to a richness and newness of life, participating in the life of the age to come, the life we will fully know and live when He comes and reigns on the new earth under the new heavens. We will know as we are 'fully known' (1 Corinthians 13:12) and, crucially, He wants to teach us how to live that life now. The kind of revelation and understanding I am talking about is more akin to knowing through experience, as if immersed in it. I may be able to quantify an ocean intellectually, but I can only know it by swimming in it and enjoying it!

Relationship is at the heart and the essence of the Trinity, and so we can confidently say that relationship, more than intellectual ability, is what God desires. Jesus taught us to know and address God as Father, which in itself is a powerful confirmation that a relationship with

---

[37] Matthew 5:17.

God is what matters. The yoke we are searching for must be relational rather than intellectual, or indeed, for that matter, industrial or work-based. It is from a revelation of relationship that we are invited into this actual vital relationship with God. We like to learn new things, which so often can pass as spiritual growth but is not necessarily relationship. In learning, I may know more about a subject and about the meaning of such and such a word (even in the original Greek!), and in knowing more in this way we can think we are growing in our faith, while all we are doing is growing in our knowledge.

Robert Harris notes, 'Men mistook measuring for understanding, always having to put themselves at the centre of everything.'[38] When we prioritise knowledge over relationship, we distance ourselves from God. Richard Rohr comments that the opposite of faith is not doubt, but certainty. In his book *The Divine Dance* he says that the life of faith is not about believing impossible things to be true but about learning to rest in infinite love.[39] We reduce faith to certainties, but the mystery of the Trinitarian God is the opposite. We seek explanation and logic, believing that reasoned arguments lead to faith, or even replace it. We saw previously that Jesus was clearly saying that the age of John the Baptist – ie the Law and the Prophets and the remarkable people who were part of that – was coming to an end, to make way for something new. The time of measuring, comparing, weighing and counting is over, not because it was wrong, but because it

---

[38] Robert Harris, *Pompeii*, New York: Random House, 2003.
[39] Richard Rohr, The *Divine Dance*, London: SPCK, 2016, p 96. My paraphrase.

pointed to something incomparably better, which has now come.

Jesus talks of His yoke being easy and light; He talks about learning from Him, and we rightly think that will include an intellectual element, but that is not the focus. If His yoke is easy and light, being one that children can know, then it is more akin to a child knowing that they are loved by their parent than knowing a set of facts about them. Knowing all about someone does not mean that you actually know them and have a living relationship with them.

If we continue our thinking of a work-based relationship, then to be pulling a plough with Jesus is impossible work and an immeasurable load. Many of us still struggle under impossible loads, imposed not by Jesus but by ourselves and others. Jesus made a point in Matthew of saying that the Pharisees were good at doing that:

> The teachers of the law and the Pharisees sit in Moses' seat. So you must be careful to do everything they tell you. But do not do what they do, for they do not practise what they preach. They tie up heavy, cumbersome loads and put them on other people's shoulders, but they themselves are not willing to lift a finger to move them.
> (Matthew 23:2-4)

I have seen so many pastors and believers burn out, fall away, lose marriages, etc, because they are trying to carry an impossible load imposed by themselves and others, with the added whisper of the accuser in the background egging them on: 'You need to do more; you just don't measure up.' We like the idea of working with Jesus as it makes us feel special, useful and significant, but that is simply setting ourselves up for a fall. The traditional image of a pair of oxen pulling a plough does not fit; the idea of Jesus on one side and us on the other does not fit at all.

False self, true self

The infinite grace found in the truth that 'the gift is not like the trespass', and that it cannot be compared, frees us from comparisons and enables us to be ourselves; I can be the real me. Knowing who I really am and being at peace in that is something we all hunger for and seek. What a wonderful gift it is to know the real authentic me. In the passage in Romans 5, Paul talks about the gift in relation to who we are and that sin has robbed us of our identity, as it did with Adam and Eve, but the gift of grace restores it.

Trappist monk Thomas Merton explored this idea and coined the phrase 'true self and false self'.[40] False self is the image of ourselves that we create to please and be acceptable to ourselves, to others and even to God. It is false because it is not who we are, but an image of the person we think we should (and ought to) be, to be valued, liked and respected. We work hard at this but it is an insatiable master, as the more we feed this image, the more it demands. If you go to any supermarket or bookstore and look at the magazines and books on sale, it is quickly self-evident that this need to build an acceptable image is

---

[40] Thomas Merton, 1915–68.

dominant in our culture. I think it has always been this way and can be traced back to the dawn of time, as it is part of the human condition. The true self is what we see when we read that 'Adam and his wife were both naked, and they felt no shame' (Genesis 2:25). Adam and Eve did not have to pretend to be anything other than who they had been created to be before God and each other. They knew they were loved and had worth just by being themselves in relation to a loving God.

The false self is who or what you present to the world which is an illusion, according to Merton, as it is outside the reach of God. Your true self is the person you are before God, that which is made in the image and likeness of God. The person that we create is false; it cannot in reality exist because it is an invention made by ourselves, others and culture, based on expectations and false comparisons.

Do you recognise the word 'comparisons'? An identity based on comparing myself with others and their expectations is an identity firmly rooted in the gift being like the trespass, which in reality is no gift at all but simply the predictable consequence of sin.

Tragically, God cannot love that person, because that person is an illusion and is a false self. It's not that God does not love the person, but that the person rooted in the false self cannot receive this love.[41] To be unknown by God is tragic. My false and private self is the one who wants to exist outside the reach of God's love and God's will, which is outside of reality and the life-giving relationship. Such an image of self cannot help but be an illusion, contrasting

---

[41] See Isaiah 59:1-2.

to the true self, which is the real and naked me. This is the life lived in the confidence of being loved, being more than enough, with no need to pretend or put on a face to myself, to others, to the world and to God. Being content with who I truly am.

We are not very good at recognising illusions, least of all the ones we cherish about ourselves; the ones we are born with and which in many ways feed the roots of sin. For many, there is no greater reality than the false self they have manufactured which cannot have a future. Maybe one of the deepest definitions of sin is a life lived outside a life-giving relationship with God. The life of the false self is a hungry one which can never be fully satisfied, like an addiction. The more I live into this, the more I need to do to keep up this façade, the more armour I need to wear to protect it and, as I clothe myself with yet more armour, it gets heavier to bear and so I need more and yet more. An ever-increasing amount of energy is spent on maintaining this self-view which is entirely based on a comparison and a lie that I am not enough. This is a brutal yoke and so far removed from the one Jesus longs to give.

As with all living things, death eventually must happen, which ultimately reveals what the life lived has been based on. Time has run out and the false self which has been nurtured all those years is revealed for what it is. The tragedy of this is described by Merton: when all is said and done, and pretence is stripped away, after I have lived my life, nothing will remain but my own naked emptiness, telling me that I am my own mistake.[42]

---

[42] Thomas Merton, *New Seeds of Contemplation*, New York: New Directions Publishing, 2007. My paraphrase.

When I was a teenager on mission one summer in the west of Scotland, we were having lunch in a small café, sheltering from the Scottish weather. There was an older German lady at the next table who we learned was a philosopher and a Christian. What an opportunity to ask some deep questions that a teenager would want to ask. I was reading Jean-Paul Satre at the time and trying to understand existentialism (I never did), so we asked about the meaning of life and of self, in relation to our young faith. She held up her hand and with her forefinger extended straight and then bent, she demonstrated that when the 'I' of self bows before Christ and so becomes a 'C', the individual is still present but finds fulfilment and identity in the 'C' of Christ. A chance encounter lasting thirty minutes shaped my life.

The cycle of grace which we will look at later comes forcefully into play. The world and its systems built on the false self say that it's what I do that matters and is the source of my significance. The gift of God's grace says my significance is who I am, and then what I do flows naturally from that. The former way of thinking is a relentless taskmaster which is never satisfied. God does not love that which is not us; He loves who I am, as I am, naked and unashamed.

C S Lewis, in his sermon *The Weight of Glory*, talks about being freed from the miserable illusion that is our doing, and rejoicing in the freedom of who we are created to be, forever being rid of our inferiority complex.[43] Paul realised and deeply understood this through his encounter with the risen Christ, that in reality, his false self image was of

---

[43] C S Lewis, *The Weight of Glory*, New York: HarperCollins, 2001.

no value. In Philippians, he says that it was worthless, comparing it to garbage:

> If someone else thinks they have reasons to put confidence in the flesh, I have more: circumcised on the eighth day, of the people of Israel, of the tribe of Benjamin, a Hebrew of Hebrews; in regard to the law, a Pharisee; as for zeal, persecuting the church; as for righteousness based on the law, faultless.
> But whatever were gains to me I now consider loss for the sake of Christ. What is more, I consider everything a loss because of the surpassing worth of knowing Christ Jesus my Lord, for whose sake I have lost all things. I consider them garbage, that I may gain Christ and be found in him, not having a righteousness of my own that comes from the law, but that which is through faith in Christ – the righteousness that comes from God on the basis of faith.
> (Philippians 3:4-9)

He had resolved not to play the game of comparisons but rather to be reconciled to who he was in Christ; to be simply loved by God, naked and unashamed, was enough. He says elsewhere, 'I care very little if I am judged by you or by any human court; indeed, I do not even judge myself' (1 Corinthians 4:3). Paul rejoices in being free from comparison, free from the law and living in the freedom of 'true self', not having to prove anything or measure up to his own or others' expectations. He calls them, too, to be free from this yoke: 'It is for freedom that Christ has set us free. Stand firm, then, and do not let yourselves be burdened again by a yoke of slavery' (Galatians 5:1).

Comparing ourselves with others is a pointless exercise, for a number of reasons. First, we do not and cannot know everything about that person, why they are like they are and who they are, as each one of us has a unique personality shaped by all of life's experiences. Second, each one of us has a unique, God-given calling, gifting and ministry, for which we are answerable to God. We are not answerable or accountable for someone else's walk with God. Third, the other person to whom we may compare ourselves is 'all used up' and the only person available for us to be is, ourselves! Colossians 1:20 talks about all things being reconciled by the blood of the cross, and so we are called to reconcile ourselves to who we are.

I recall waking up one morning with the words, 'Learn to live with your humanity,' going around in my head. God was speaking to me about my striving for perfection and comparing myself to others and the need to be reconciled to who I was in Him. I was called to be who I was, not what someone else was.

Jesus has laid an axe to the root of comparisons of any kind, setting us free from the tyranny of performance-based life and religion. What a gift of grace and, indeed, 'the gift is not like the trespass'!

Summary

In the gift of grace, which cannot be compared to the trespass, God does a new thing that frees us from the need to compare ourselves with others and be something other than who we are. We are invited to rest and be reconciled to who we are, deeply loved by God and of infinite value. Jesus has for all time broken the yoke of performance-based religion, setting us free to follow Him and accept His gift of grace in a new, life-giving way.

You can begin to see why I consider that the concept of a wooden-like, work-based yoke, however snuggly it fits, simply does not square with the flow and direction of Scripture. Jesus, in talking about rest for our souls, calls for an end to lives spent under the tyranny of comparison, continually working and trying to be something which we are not. He invites us to stop working for something which is a fabrication and is born from separation from God and not in grace. This surely is good news!

It really is time for something new.

Waymarker

Sit
Find somewhere comfortable where you can spend some time in undisturbed prayer and reflection. Breathe deeply and relax in the knowledge that you have nothing to prove and can simply be yourself in this space. If it would help, you could imagine yourself being held in the love of God, like being in a warm sea.

Reflect
Comparing yourself to others is usually a downward spiral. To have someone as a mentor, a spiritual companion[44] or an example can be inspiring, but always so

---

[44] Simply put, a spiritual companion is someone who supports you in your spiritual growth, helping you to navigate your beliefs, encouraging and offering non-directional insights, so that you can deepen your understanding of yourself. A spiritual director is

that you can be your authentic self and not a cut-down version of them.

What would it mean for you to be reconciled to who you are and the gifts and ministry that God has given you? Ask God to show you your true self and how He sees and values you in that way.

Pray

Ask God to show you who you really are in His sight, and His love for you. Speak to Him about how you have seen yourself and ask Him to forgive you for these false images. These images are not how He sees you. Take time to stop and, in prayer, without words, simply rest in His love.

---

someone who is more proactive and directive in helping you in your faith journey.

6
Jesus' yoke

> If you can't explain it simply, you don't understand it well enough.
> *Albert Einstein*[45]

Jesus' teaching, simple but not simplistic

In many ways, you could say that Jesus' teaching was simple, but certainly not simplistic. We have probably all found that frequently the best solution to a difficult problem is the simplest one. Jesus said that even the little ones could enter the kingdom,[46] which means that the solution really does have to be straightforward, simple and accessible to everyone, including children, the outcasts and those that mainstream society, particularly the religious elite, consider to be outsiders. These are the ones who in reality grasped the essentials of the kingdom first.

When we consider the context in which Jesus was teaching and what He is inviting us into, we need to

---

[45] www.brainyquote.com/quotes/albert_einstein_383803 (accessed 4th April 2025).
[46] Matthew 18:3.

approach it from a different perspective. In Ephesians, a sharp contrast between faith and works is made:

> For it is by grace you have been saved, through faith
> – and this is not from yourselves, it is the gift of God
> – not by works, so that no one can boast.
> (Ephesians 2:8-9)

We no longer come from the old and tired way of works, which is the way of my own achievements, whatever that may look like, but from the completely different approach of faith. It has very little to do with us and a lot to do with Him, as it's a free gift graciously given. Our part to play in this transaction is to accept it with thankfulness.

Too full to learn

There is an old tale, of uncertain origins,[47] of a wise teacher who was highly respected. Seekers from far and wide would journey to sit at his feet and drink from the well of his insight.

One day, a distinguished young man arrived. 'I wish to learn from you,' he declared. 'Open my mind and show me new truths.' His voice carried the weight of self-assurance, the bearing of one long used to command. The teacher welcomed him with a gentle smile and invited him to share tea.

As the tea was being made, the visitor spoke at length of his triumphs, his studies, his gifts and his vast

---

[47] See www.thetcacupoflife.com/2015/06/the-tale-of-overflowing-teacup.html (accessed 7th April 2025). There are many varying accounts of this story online.

understanding. Word upon word flowed from him, a stream of self-praise seeking validation.

At last, the tea was ready and the teacher began to pour. The cup was filled and still he poured. Tea spilled into the saucer and then onto the young man's robes. 'Enough!' the visitor cried. 'The cup is already full!'

The teacher paused and looked at him with calm eyes. 'Indeed,' he said softly. 'This cup is you, brimming over with your own knowledge and opinions. There is no space left for anything new. Return when your cup is empty, when your mind is open and you are ready to truly listen.'

Is this what Jesus meant when he said, 'Blessed are the poor in spirit' (Matthew 5:3), or spoke about the little ones coming to him?[48] In a tragic twist, the man who thought he was wise lacked spiritual understanding, but he did not and could not recognise that. It is only when we have an open attitude that it is possible to learn anything. Actually, it is being wise enough to realise that I don't know it all.

We project our opinionated, fractured mindset and expectations onto Jesus and His teaching, assuming we know how things should work, and onto God, in how we think He should be. God created us in His image,[49] and we have returned the compliment! Dr Stephen Kershaw, a University of Oxford-based palaeontologist, commented that 'we read, understand and reconstitute the past in our cultural present which often tells as much about ourselves as the past we are looking at. We are telling about

---

[48] Mark 10:14.
[49] Genesis 1:27.

ourselves when we think we are talking about them.'[50] We read into what Jesus is saying from our own cultural bias, which in this instance is one that says that our value comes from work, in 'pulling our own weight', earning our keep and so gaining self-worth. But we can be so full of our own opinions that we can't hear the Master speak!

Jesus came to make what we don't understand understandable and to turn our upside-down thinking the right way up. He challenges us to realise that our worth has nothing to do with how hard we work or how much we know, but all to do with how much we are loved. In our hearts, we like and entertain the idea that we are loved and accepted unconditionally, but in practice we find this very hard to accept. So often our sense of self-worth is based on what we do and can bring and is so deeply ingrained that it is hard to let go.

Jesus always moves towards the broken, never drawing back in revulsion as He touches and embraces us, physically then, and emotionally and spiritually now. He never takes a stand-offish, one-step-removed attitude. On the cross, He fully embraced all of us as humanity – as we as individuals come to Him in faith, He embraces all of our sinfulness. He embraces all of us, every last atom of who you and I are. We can be uncomfortable with this as we prefer a working relationship, albeit a benign, loving and forgiving one. We prefer our terms and our status rather than simply yielding all. I fear that much of the Church also finds this a more comfortable approach to God.

---

[50] Dr Stephen Kershaw, BBC Radio 4, *You're Dead to Me*, broadcast 27th July 2024), www.bbc.co.uk/sounds/play/m0021h3v (accessed 4th April 2025).

Included

We read that we are 'united', 'included', raised up and seated with Christ 'in the heavenly realms' (Philippians 2:1; Ephesians 1:13; Ephesians 2:6). We are called to be in a deeply intimate relationship with Him. And it's a reciprocal relationship.

> Jesus replied, 'Anyone who loves me will obey my teaching. My Father will love them, and we will come to them and make our home with them.'
> (John 14:23)

It is a strange thought that God should make His home in us, in you and me. God is 'at home' in us! If God is 'at home' in us, then should we not be 'at home' in ourselves, comfortable in our own skin, rather than accepting the self-loathing and rejection many of us feel? Jesus has given us the gift of being at peace with God and with ourselves. We can read on in Scripture, emphasising and even expanding on this:

> But now he has reconciled you by Christ's physical body through death to present you holy in his sight, without blemish and free from accusation.
> (Colossians 1:22)

> Therefore, if anyone is in Christ, the new creation has come: the old has gone, the new is here! All this is from God, who reconciled us to himself through Christ and gave us the ministry of reconciliation: that God was reconciling the world to himself in Christ, not counting people's sins against them.
> (2 Corinthians 5:17-19)

What an incredible paradigm shift; we now find ourselves part of this new creation, reconciled, the old has gone. We have already read that the relationship with God through Christ is a close, intimate one. Thoughts and ideas of a working relationship involving ideas akin to a wooden yoke seem, once again, not to be a fitting analogy.

There must be another biblical understanding, in keeping with Jesus' teaching and the thinking of that day.

Rabbi's yoke

Earlier, we saw that the rabbi's yoke was the interpretation of how the rabbi understood and applied the Torah. Jesus' words in Matthew 11 need to be understood in this context. Fourteen times in the New Testament Jesus is referred to as a rabbi, but not like other rabbis, as He taught with real authority and not as the others taught.[51] His calling of His followers was not based on selecting the most suitable; rather, it seemed at times to be the opposite! Ability, intellect, gender, wealth or age didn't seem to come into it; rather, the completely different basis of faith. Most of those called were already back in village life following ordinary occupations; they had not made the grade, and yet Jesus was calling them to be His disciples. On the day Jesus came along, saying to them to come and follow Him, they left their boats as they were given a second chance by this different rabbi, with a different understanding of Torah.[52] This rabbi doesn't call the best to be His disciples but calls those who have been rejected by others.

---

[51] Matthew 7:29; Mark 1:22; John 3:2.
[52] Matthew 4:19.

We have the words of this rabbi calling all those who are weary and carrying heavy burdens, who are worn down by the cares of life, who have not made the grade, are not clever enough and not rich enough. Not the sort of people that the other rabbis were looking for, and not just males! He utters the call of the rabbi:

> Come to me, all you who are weary and burdened, and I will give you rest. Take my yoke upon you [*my interpretation of the Torah*] and learn from me, for I am gentle and humble in heart [*as is my Father*], and you will find rest for your souls [*not the misery of trying to live out complex laws. Why?*]. For my yoke is easy and my burden is light.
> (Matthew 11:28-30)

By saying that His yoke 'is easy', Jesus does not mean that living according to His interpretation of the law is easy with no challenges, but that it is different. Jesus is not a rabbi who engages in all sorts of legalistic gymnastics, but is one who preaches with authority; He teaches clearly and boldly the good news of the kingdom of God. We don't need to be anyone special to be His disciples as He calls all of us out of our ordinary, often burdensome, lives and offers us the chance to find the way to God through faith in Him and by learning from His teaching.

Jesus says that He has fulfilled the law, making all things new with His interpretation and application of the Torah, which is breathtakingly radical. So radical that the religious leaders of His day reject Him and His teaching completely.

No one had come like Jesus, with no one before Jesus knowing and bringing the message that Jesus did. No one knew the Father like the Son, no one else had been at creation, at the giving of the law, and no one else had come like this to make it known.

Simply replacing one yoke of slavery, Egyptian, Babylonian or otherwise with another, does not do justice to what Jesus is saying. It isn't good enough, nor is it radical enough; it merely reworks the same old, tired thinking. This kind of image doesn't reflect our relationship with Jesus. So, if that isn't how we interact with Him, we must ask: What is?

The answer has already been given: 'Believe' (John 6:29). Just believe. Jesus said that believing is like being a child, knowing the Father in the way a child knows their parent.[53] It's not about studying Him or knowing facts about Him, but actually knowing Him. That's how His kingdom works.

In contrast, the Pharisees responded to questions about religious observance and knowing God by prescribing more work, more burdens and more effort. They created all sorts of inventive ways to try to win God's approval through sheer exertion. I've seen this, heard it and felt it time and again. The apostles encountered the same mindset when dealing with believers who came from the party of the Pharisees:

> Now then, why do you try to test God by putting on the necks of Gentiles a yoke that neither we nor our ancestors have been able to bear? No! We believe it

---

[53] My paraphrase of Matthew 18:2-5 and Mark 10:14-16.

is through the grace of our Lord Jesus that we are saved, just as they are.
(Acts 15:10-11)

They knew that the way forward, which was the way Jesus had started, was not to put those burdens and expectations on people again. Whenever a yoke is talked about, it often seems to be in a negative sense, involving work or performance of some kind; seemingly that is what we are hard-wired to think.

Jesus' perspective

You have been very patient, as it has taken time to lay the necessary foundation, but finally we can now ask, what does Jesus mean by His yoke? If we want an image to help us understand, we need something better than a piece of wood. When Jesus talks of a yoke, He comes from a completely different perspective, which is a place of grace, rest, freedom and love. We know that 'the law was given through Moses; grace and truth came through Jesus Christ' (John 1:17), so something different is being spoken about, as the law is a heavy yoke. Love, grace and truth are light and completely different from the traditional understanding of Torah, and Jesus explicitly goes beyond this.

What, then, is Jesus' yoke? Jesus brings a fresh understanding of the Torah, taking it back to its essentials, which are again straightforward and simple. Matthew, Mark and Luke record Jesus' answer to a question about the law and which commandment is most important. Mark records:

'The most important one,' answered Jesus, 'is this: "Hear, O Israel: the Lord our God, the Lord is one. Love the Lord your God with all your heart and with all your soul and with all your mind and with all your strength." The second is this: "Love your neighbour as yourself." There is no commandment greater than these.'
(Mark 12:29-31)[54]

Jesus cuts through all the myriads of laws, boiling it down to love: love of God and love of neighbour. To love, one must know love.

Laws don't teach love or show love, as they are cold and impersonal. We cannot know a loving God who calls us to love by keeping rules. We have seen that religious observance had got to an absurd level, clearly was not working and had failed badly.

I have met so many Christians who feel like failures because they don't think they read their Bibles enough, don't pray enough, find it difficult to memorise Scripture and struggle to attend prayer meetings after a long and taxing day at work. In short, Christians who don't do what they feel is expected of them.

Jesus' yoke is very simple yet so profound. So straightforward that even the little ones, those of us who are foolish in the eyes of the world, can grasp it.[55]

Jesus' yoke is simply the yoke which Jesus had and knew Himself, which He lived into and continually experienced. The yoke He grew up with is seen when at

---

[54] Also Matthew 22:37-40, Luke 10:27.
[55] 1 Corinthians 1:25 talks about 'the foolishness of God' being 'wiser than human wisdom'.

twelve years old He went to the temple to be in His 'Father's house' (Luke 2:49), and later became clear at His baptism when a voice from heaven said, 'This is my Son, whom I love; with him I am well pleased' (Matthew 3:17).

Jesus' yoke, the yoke under which He Himself lived, was not the yoke of the Torah, of Mosaic Law or of human expectation or fabrication, but was His Father's embrace.

If you think about it, a yoke is something carried around the neck; it is a burden. But is not an embrace also carried around the neck? An embrace, by contrast, is a tangible expression of love and acceptance. Jesus knew and experienced the love of His Father. Though it was not physical, it was profoundly real to Him. He accepted that embrace and lived in it, continually leaning into it. Often, He would go alone to a quiet place to renew and refresh that connection. In knowing and living into this yoke of the Father's embrace, Jesus met the demands of the law from a place of love. The impersonal demands of the law were and are always fulfilled by love!

We can go further in understanding Jesus' yoke that He carried and even rejoiced in. In the middle of His earthly life, challenges and trials and ultimately His passion, what was the yoke that made it easy and light? The yoke that Jesus gladly bore was the Father's pleasure, the Father's embrace, which was a 'joy ... set before him' (Hebrews 12:2).

This yoke connected Father and Son in an intimate, loving way. That embrace which Jesus knew most certainly was not a working relationship, but as He clearly spoke of, was one of sonship. It was not only the Father's embrace, it was also the Trinity, the community of God embracing Jesus. Jesus Christ was and is fully human and fully God. I have no wish to enter into a detailed discussion on the Trinity, as other minds better than mine have and will continue to debate this, but as the 'Christ', He had known and will continue to know from and for all eternity what it is to be part of that loving, embracing community. Following His baptism, if not before, Jesus was aware of this divine embrace, the Father, the Son and the Holy Spirit, defining who He was and in which He had identity and purpose.

The yoke that Jesus bore was the Godhead embracing and approving, the Father saying, 'This is my beloved Son,'[56] and the Holy Spirit's active presence guiding, supporting and leading. When Jesus says for us to take His yoke upon us as it is easy and will bring rest, He is referring to this divine embrace. He wants us to know for ourselves and, indeed, He came to make this possible, the Father's embrace, that 'I love you for who you are not what you have done'.

> The Father himself loves you because you have loved me and have believed that I came from God. (John 16:27)

When we can experience the loving embrace and acceptance of God, why on earth do we want to even entertain the idea of the distance that a wooden bar would bring between us? Does the idea of God embracing us make us feel so uncomfortable that we want a space between us? Does the idea of being brought intimately into the community of God, the Trinity, frighten us?

---

[56] See Matthew 3:17.

The work of the cross, that yoke of wood which Jesus bore, was that we could be free from it.

Jesus took the wood so we could take His embrace.

A powerful example

When we look at the opening verse to the parables in Luke 15, we see that Jesus' answer was in response to the Pharisees' mutterings about why He welcomed sinners and even ate with them. Jesus told these three stories as one parable. One parable in which the lost sheep was carried on the shepherd's shoulders, the lost coin held tightly in the widow's hand and the lost son embraced in his father's arms. We wonder if the older son would know the father's embrace as well, as we are left hanging, pondering how the story will end.

In the parable of the prodigal son, Jesus spells out in a compelling story the difference between the old way of thinking and the new understanding He is bringing. He explains why the old way is dead and no longer works, with the Pharisees asking, so to speak, why more people want to follow Jesus than them. Jesus explains why in this parable and so we see a perfect illustration of this new understanding of yoke. In this wonderful passage, Jesus goes deeper than almost anywhere else to give an understanding of the relationship between humanity and God as our heavenly Father. It is as though Jesus, in telling this parable, is pulling back a curtain to reveal some very deep insights.[57]

---

[57] For a deeper commentary and understanding of this passage, see Kenneth E Bailey, *Poet & Peasant* and *Through Peasant Eyes*, Combined Edition, Grand Rapids, MI: William B Eerdmans Publishing Co, 1990.

After his tragic leaving, the son turned back to go home to his father with the prepared script:

> Father, I have sinned against heaven and against you. I am no longer worthy to be called your son; make me like one of your hired servants.
> (Luke 15:18-19)

You can imagine the son rehearsing these words as he trudged home. First, hoping that he would even get to see his father. Second, that the father would actually listen to him, which was far from guaranteed; and third, of course, that the father would graciously agree to the terms of return that the son was suggesting. It is striking that the son never got to say the final phrase, about being 'like one of your hired servants'. He either gave up, seeing no point in the face of such extravagant love, or his father simply would not allow him to finish his prepared speech as he embraced him. The first thing the father did was to run to meet the son, throw his arms around him and kiss him. He silenced the questions and even the accusation that a rebellious son is to be stoned at the city gates (Deuteronomy 21:18-21). The father answered all the questions the son had, and the questions the village and the estate workers would have had as well, about how the son should be received.

The son wanted to negotiate the terms of their relationship, to have control of it and to have some say as to how it was going to work out. The father was having none of that!

Nouwen, *Return of the Prodigal*. Tim Keller, *The Prodigal God*, London: Hodder & Stoughton, 2009.

What a surprise the son got. No wooden yoke, working to repay his debt or a set of scales to compare himself, but a completely different kind of yoking and joining. He never even had a chance to complete his prepared speech! He only got as far as saying he had sinned against his father and against heaven, which was certainly true as, when he originally left home, he showed incredible disrespect and brought shame on his father and family by wanting his share of the inheritance now. He was in effect wanting his father dead.

Now, on his return, he wanted to say that he was no longer worthy to be called his son. Aware of the vast debt he owed, he was ready to go on to say he would work as a hired hand, taking his father's agricultural or industrial yoke upon himself. I think he must have been shocked to the core when his father responded by throwing his arms around him. The yoke the son had been expecting was the work of a wooden farm implement, but the yoke he received was a massive embrace! In addition to the embrace, we read of even greater intimacy and acceptance; as if to prove the point, the father kissed the son.

The father took the shame so the son could take the embrace.

It is not that after this the son did not work on the father's farm and in the father's business. Of course he did! But he worked as a son and not as a servant. He worked from a completely different perspective. He didn't work for wages because he had no option, but he worked because he wanted to. Can you imagine the joy in his life as he got out of bed facing each day's toil? He would sweat and grunt with the best of the hired hands, but the motivation was entirely different. He was coming from a place of love and embrace, which made his work a pleasure. He truly had peace, he truly knew rest, he knew who he was, he knew he was loved, he knew he was fully accepted and he knew that whatever debt he had owed to his father was fully forgiven and paid. Rest to his soul in a very real and practical life-giving way! The prodigal son knew the yoke of the father's embrace while the older son only knew the yoke of the toil in his father's house.

Childlikeness

Jesus welcomed little children, as we read:

> People were also bringing babies to Jesus for him to place his hands on them. When the disciples saw this, they rebuked them. But Jesus called the children to him and said, 'Let the little children come to me, and do not hinder them, for the kingdom of God belongs to such as these. Truly I tell you, anyone who will not receive the kingdom of God like a little child will never enter it.'
> (Luke 18:15-17)

Jesus accepts and lays His hands on the children in a loving, calm, accepting way, and says clearly that this is how you come, this is how you enter. As adults, we can entertain the idea of a yoke in the traditional working sense, but is this appropriate for little children? Doing chores and working as part of the family was expected and normal, as it is often today, but the idea of exploitation abuse and slavery most certainly was not in Jesus' mind. However, this loving embrace is the kind that a child can understand, even while the wise and learned may struggle with it.

It's similar to the chat Jesus had with Nicodemus in John 3 about going back to another kind of embrace which is even more intimate: his mother's womb! Jesus was inviting Nicodemus to know the very birthplace of all life, in creation and in our lives as individuals, which is found within the dynamic loving relationship of the Trinity.

When a child comes of age there are, of course, responsibilities that come with it. We are children and God wants us to mature into adults joining in with Him in His work, and not seeing ourselves as servants or slaves simply drawing our wages with no responsibility other than turning up for work and discharging our duties. When we are embraced by God, as the prodigal was by his father on his return, there is a change in the relationship; no longer simply working for recompense as the older son thought, but a relationship transformed to one of trust and responsibility. The Father's business is now your business and you have a share in it.

God's heart

This parable in Luke 15 is a deep revelation of the heart of God. It is a deep insight into the nature of God, brought by the Son. In returning to our original passage in Matthew 11:29, Jesus also gives an intimate insight into His heart. He says that his heart is 'gentle and lowly' (ESV), which in effect is saying that His very nature is gentle and lowly, especially to those seeking Him, those who are heavy laden and burdened. I believe this is the only passage where Jesus tells us about His own heart.[58] By heart, I am not referring to the emotional life, but the centre of all we are and do and our motivation. This is who Jesus is, lowly and humble, approachable, appreciating others and not lording it over them.

Jesus, though, is certainly not all warm and fuzzy; for example; He is exacting in His denouncing of Chorazin and Bethsaida in Matthew 11:21. The haughty and proud exclude themselves, yet the young child is welcome and sees, understands and even is embraced by Jesus![59]

To return to Luke 15 and the account of the lost sheep, the lost coin and the lost son, the very thing that qualified them to be embraced was that they had got lost in the first place! Our very lostness and burden is what qualifies us to come. Getting lost and realising this, as the younger son did, is all that is needed to be found. And not only being found, but embraced. Jesus never tires of sweeping us into His tender embrace!

We have all heard many anecdotes of Jesus as a carpenter making yokes, the best of the lot and perfectly fitting, and yet it is strange how we prefer the anecdote rather than what the Bible says. We take the idea of yoke as depicted in the Old Testament but fail to realise that God has done a new thing.

From rabbi to rabboni

We read of Mary and Martha in the well-known domestic scene in Bethany:

---

[58] Dane Ortland, *Gentle and Lowly: The Heart of Christ for Sinners and Sufferers*, Wheaton, IL: Crossway, 2020, p 18.
[59] Psalm 10.25-28.

> He [Jesus] came to a village where a woman named Martha opened her home to him. She had a sister called Mary, who sat at the Lord's feet listening to what he said. But Martha was distracted by all the preparations that had to be made. She came to him and asked, 'Lord, don't you care that my sister has left me to do the work by myself? Tell her to help me!'
> 'Martha, Martha,' the Lord answered, 'you are worried and upset about many things, but few things are needed – or indeed only one. Mary has chosen what is better, and it will not be taken away from her.
> (Luke 10:38-42)

One of the traditional ways of seeing this passage is as a discussion on personality types, the active and the contemplative. Tom Wright suggests that the viewpoint of the listeners at the time was that Mary was in the man's place.[60] The clearly defined cultural norms of male and female were being broken by Mary as she sat at Jesus' feet, not necessarily looking up adoringly, but actually learning as she was putting herself in a disciple's place, which in that culture at that time was exclusively male. Paul sat at the teacher Gamaliel's feet, probably not as an adoring admirer, but as a student. No wonder Martha was stressed. It wasn't just the work that she had to do; it was also that Mary was flagrantly breaking all the cultural norms.

I once felt a failure at not being able to recall and remember all that God had taught me and the Scripture I

---

[60] Tom Wright, *Luke for Everyone*, London: SPCK, 2001, p 130.

had learned. The Lord clearly impressed on me a question: 'Do you want to know all the facts, to have perfect recall, or do you want to know the Lord of the facts, who can bring what you have learned to mind when you need it?' I sensed He was asking me if I wanted to be a disciple investing in a life-giving relationship, or to focus on sterile, intellectual knowledge. Unsurprisingly, I chose the life-giving relationship option! It's the relationship that brings life, not knowledge.

Jesus teaches us how to live in His embrace, knowing the life-giving relationship with Him. On Easter morning we read that Mary called the resurrected Jesus 'Rabboni', meaning 'Teacher' (John 20:16). Jesus saved and delivered Mary from her life of sin, yet when she met Him, she called Him 'Rabboni' – Teacher, not Saviour – though He clearly was. Jesus taught and still teaches His disciples how to live by grace in His embrace, which is a burden that is light. And so Mary met Jesus in the garden on His resurrection and said, 'Rabboni [my Teacher].' Jesus taught her to live. He set her free from so much, but He also taught her to live in that freedom. Jesus wants to instruct us how to live into His teaching of grace, to live into that vital life-giving relationship of who we are as God's children.

Identity assault

It was not on the miracles that Jesus did, but on His identity that the devil attacked Jesus. The temptations in the wilderness[61] and the insults of the Pharisees were based on the question, 'Who do you think you are?' It is the same with us. The devil is adept at challenging us on

---

[61] See Matthew 4:1-11; Luke 4:1-13.

our identity as children embraced by God, using his often and well-used line that we all know: 'Who do think you are? You call yourself a Christian?' We listen to this and resort to the safe relationship of a working yoke, as it responds to that accusation, feeds on our insecurities and keeps us in bondage to that yoke of having always to prove ourselves. It can be easier in the short term to lie down and give up!

This is exactly where the devil wants us and precisely what Jesus came to free us from. The task for us is not to earn our salvation but to be secure in who we are, in our Father's love for us, in the sufficiency of Jesus' sacrifice. To put that insecurity and condemnation to rest and to start to live from a place of security that Jesus teaches us to live in.

Rublev, in his fifteenth-century icon, gives a helpful image depicting the Trinity seated around three sides of a table with the fourth side open to the viewer.[62] There is a mark on the front of the table which is thought to be where a mirror was once placed. The mirror reflected the viewer and so included them in the holy group seated around the table. Rublev is drawing the onlooker into the table and into the divine community. The space and aspect of the icon is deliberately left open, emphasising that this is an open and welcoming place in which there is a place for us and to which we are welcome.

---

[62] *Trinity*, Andrei Rublev. A simple Google search will show many coloured images. An icon is not something that is to be worshipped but a means to understand and access what it represents.

Jesus knew the embrace of the Father and accordingly also the Trinity. He was, and knew Himself to be, a vital part of that divine, life-giving community. In the embrace we are talking about, we are firmly invited and included in this community, the very heart of God. This is a yoke which is *you*-shaped, Jesus-shaped and God-shaped! A natural organic fit with you as a child, but which grows with you as you grow up and mature into Christ. As we grow up in Him, so this image can change and grow with us. This yoke is not a thing to pull but an embrace to rest into.

Discipleship is more than a six-week course about doctrine, but can rather be seen as a divine embrace into which we can relax and get comfortable. The areas that are uncomfortable and awkward need to move to allow the embrace to be closer; we adjust ourselves until we are absolutely comfortable, at ease and at home in the Father's embrace. The sadness a parent feels when they want to embrace their child to comfort and console them but they squirm or run away, hiding and refusing the comfort offered. Tragically I wonder if we can also run and hide from God's embrace. Going back to the parable of the prodigal son, the joy of the father embracing his returning younger son who finally allows Dad to embrace him is contrasted with the heartbreak when the older, distant son seems to be rejecting his father's invitation. We don't know how the story ends, but at this point we can sense the father's sadness. God is saddened when we turn our back on Him and refuse to come home, because one day there will be a reckoning when who we are and what we have built our lives on is finally revealed.

We are thinking about our identity in this section, and we are thinking again about the parable of the prodigal son and how, on returning, the son considered himself as a servant. The father's embrace forced him to rethink and realise that his identity was not as a servant but as a son. How he saw himself was radically changed, and from that profoundly changed view of himself, he would have behaved quite differently. I hope that in receiving this radical grace and forgiveness he would have been, and we would also be, gracious and generous to others.

Summary

Jesus' yoke is the embrace which He himself knew, which was the Father's and indeed the Holy Trinity's. Jesus unpacks this in the parable of the prodigal son, who came back wanting to take on a yoke of work which the father explicitly refused to give him, but instead embraced him, declaring him as his son. Jesus' yoke is what He knew and experienced. He invites us to share none other than the Father's embrace, which means that we are embraced by God – Father, Son and Holy Spirit – as a welcome member of the divine community.

Waymarker

Sit
Find a place where you can be alone and undisturbed. Settle down and relax.

Reflect
Visualise yourself as the child being embraced, enthusiastically welcomed and deeply loved by the Father. What does this feel like, and how does it change your view of God and His love for you? Don't hurry this; simply allow yourself to be embraced, and relax into it. Try not to stiffen or resist. There is nothing to be said, as this is beyond words.

Pray

Thank God for His love. Don't try to make excuses or justify yourself. There is no need; it is Jesus who justifies you. In the Lord's Prayer we first of all call Him Father, and it is only later we ask for forgiveness.

When you are ready, you can ask God to forgive and cleanse you. There is no need to agonise about this or endlessly repeat your confession. In the very act of coming, you are repenting and asking for forgiveness. Thank God for His love – that's all you have to do; the rest does not need words.

7
Through the Old Testament

'What no eye has seen,
what no ear has heard,
and what no human mind has conceived' –
the things God has prepared for those who love him.
1 Corinthians 2:9

Throughout history, humanity has struggled under various yokes, including slavery, oppression and self-imposed burdens. However, the greatest weight we carry is an internal burden of fragmentation from which the external ones derive. We trace this originally back to the Garden of Eden, which depicts that original fragmentation from God and ourselves causing the burden of sin, a burden which we were never created to bear. In this chapter, I want to explore this theme, starting with the story of Jacob and Esau, and follow its development through the Old Testament to the life of Jesus and then back to Abraham. Throughout, we see how God repeatedly breaks the yoke of bondage and leads us to true freedom.

A recurring theme

Looking at the first time a word is used in the Bible is often helpful in understanding its context. The word 'yoke' is no different, and understanding the first time it is used helps us grasp its implications and significance.

To find the first time 'yoke' is used in the Bible, we need to go back to the account of twins, Esau and Jacob, who themselves had a fragmented relationship even before they were born. Jacob was jealous of his older brother's position, wanting his birthright, which he later obtained for the price of a meal. Esau had been hunting and was famished on his return, when Jacob took the opportunity to trade Esau's birthright as oldest son for a pot of stew![63]

Later, when the time came for Isaac, their father, to give Esau the traditional oldest son's blessing, he sent him out hunting to get something tasty before he blessed him. Meanwhile Jacob, encouraged by his mother, pretended to be Esau and received the blessing instead.[64] When Esau returned and came to his father, rather than the desired blessing, Isaac instead spoke over him, 'You will live by the sword and you will serve your brother,' making Esau cry out bitterly, but his father continued with a promise: 'But when you grow restless, you will throw his yoke from off your neck' (Genesis 27:40).

From the deceit of this sad story, we learn that the first use of the word 'yoke' was in the context of subjugation and loss of birthright through deception, but importantly also that the birthright itself was held very lightly, being traded for that pot of stew, however tasty.

---

[63] Genesis 25:24-34.
[64] Genesis 27.

Many years later, when Israel found itself in a place of oppression and slavery under the harsh Egyptian yoke, with the pain finally becoming intolerable, they cried out to God, who heard their cry and set in motion His deliverance plan. God heard their cry of pain. In Exodus we have a graphic image of the yoke of slavery being broken:

> Moreover, I have heard the groaning of the Israelites, whom the Egyptians are enslaving, and I have remembered my covenant.
> Therefore, say to the Israelites: 'I am the LORD, and I will bring you out from under the yoke of the Egyptians. I will free you from being slaves to them, and I will redeem you with an outstretched arm and with mighty acts of judgment. I will take you as my own people, and I will be your God. Then you will know that I am the LORD your God, who brought you out from under the yoke of the Egyptians.
> (Exodus 6:5-7)

In the book of Judges, we see a recurring cycle in which Israel repeatedly fell under the oppressive yoke of foreign powers until their suffering became unbearable. In desperation they cried out to God, who heard them and provided deliverance. However, time and again, about twelve times in total, they found themselves back in the same predicament. This pattern continues throughout Israel's history, with God bringing them into freedom from foreign domination but they repeatedly find themselves back under a yoke of rule. The story of moving from freedom to being under a yoke becomes predictably wretched. For instance, in Numbers we read:

> While Israel was staying in Shittim, the men began to indulge in sexual immorality with Moabite women, who invited them to the sacrifices to their gods. The people ate the sacrificial meal and bowed down before these gods. So Israel yoked themselves to the Baal of Peor.
> (Numbers 25:1-3)

I find it remarkable, but so revealing, that despite the Israelites being set free from slavery, they longed to return to the certainty of what it provided. We can see this in Exodus 14:11-12,[65] which talks about their desire for the past.

I have met older people who lived in Central Asia during the Soviet era who hanker for the old times. They forget the untold hardships and millions of people who died on the whim of one man and instead recall the certainty of everything being provided and not needing to think for themselves. I wonder if, unknowingly, we long for the same, as time and time again we see this playing out – just keep us fed and comfortable and we will not ask for anything more – and slowly slide unwittingly into a place of bondage. 'Bread and circuses', as Juvenal, the second-century Roman poet, said.[66]

Esau sold his birthright for a pot of stew, Israel longed to go back to the 'pots of meat' of Egypt (Exodus 16:3) and Adam and Eve traded their inheritance for a piece of fruit! The yoke of slavery stops us from maturing to become responsible adults and instead suppresses growth and the

---

[65] See also Exodus 16:3; 17:3; Numbers 14:1-4.
[66] www.goodreads.com/quotes/10603579-give-them-bread-and-circuses-and-they-will-never-revolt (accessed 4th April 2025).

ability to think for ourselves, to be responsible for who we are. Slavery robs us of our birthright and, often, even the memory of who we really are. How many of us prefer being told what to do and think, rather than maturing and in all things growing up into Christ?[67] I believe that this lack of a maturing faith is one of the reasons that spiritual abuse is enabled by leaders over their congregations.

A subtle change

The major themes of yoke in the Old Testament are predominately about how Egypt, Babylon and other nations placed a stranglehold on Israel, by enslaving them in differing ways. In Leviticus and later in Ezekiel, as with so many other passages, a yoke directly equates to slavery:

> I am the LORD your God, who brought you out of Egypt so that you would no longer be slaves to the Egyptians; I broke the bars of your yoke and enabled you to walk with heads held high.
> (Leviticus 26:13)

> They will know that I am the LORD, when I break the bars of their yoke and rescue them from the hands of those who enslaved them.
> (Ezekiel 34:27)

Time and time again the Bible uses the idea of a yoke to describe the oppressive situation that Israel found itself in. God promised that this yoke would be removed, the yoke of foreign domination, but more than that, the yoke of whatever would oppress God's people. Many similar

---

[67] Ephesians 4:15.

prophecies were given promising that the yoke would be removed.

Isaiah and Jeremiah added their voices to this unfolding theme of yoke. In Isaiah, God promised to take the Assyrian yoke off Israel's shoulders:

> 'I will crush the Assyrian in my land;
> on my mountains I will trample him down.
> His yoke will be taken from my people,
> and his burden removed from their shoulders.'
>
> This is the plan determined for the whole world;
> this is the hand stretched out over all nations.
> (Isaiah 14:25-26)

> 'In that day,' declares the LORD Almighty,
> 'I will break the yoke off their necks
> and will tear off their bonds;
> no longer will foreigners enslave them.
> Instead, they will serve the LORD their God
> and David their king,
> whom I will raise up for them.'
> (Jeremiah 30:8-9)

We can begin to see a shift in the prophetic promise, with Isaiah extending the promise of release to the 'whole world' and Jeremiah referring to serving the Lord and 'David their king'. The reference to serving David their king – who, of course, at the time of this prophecy was firmly in the past – means that they were looking forward to the day when one of David's descendants would once again sit on David's throne. This future aspect never happened in all the Old Testament history, until the New

Testament where Matthew in his genealogy stresses that Jesus is a direct descendant of David.

Jesus as the Messiah, the One prophesied to remove the yoke, interprets this in a completely different way. He does not take on the crushing Roman domination but addresses a deeper problem, bringing a permanent solution to the dilemma of removing yokes and breaking bonds. The wonderful promise of the Messiah removing the yoke is given in Isaiah:

> For as in the day of Midian's defeat,
> you have shattered
> the yoke that burdens them,
> the bar across their shoulders,
> the rod of their oppressor. ...
> For to us a child is born,
> to us a son is given,
> and the government will be on his shoulders.
> And he will be called
> Wonderful Counsellor, Mighty God,
> Everlasting Father, Prince of Peace.
> (Isaiah 9:4,6)

The nature of the yoke of slavery had subtly changed from foreign domination to a different yoke of religious legalism. The original yoke of slavery to Egypt and other nations, from which Israel was still not free as they did not enjoy independence, had taken on a new form: the yoke of the law. They had been set free from slavery to Pharaoh, which among other things had included making clay bricks without straw. This newly formed nation of Israel was given the law on Mount Sinai as a guide in how to live as the people of God, but we see that over time they traded that for slavery to the law. The law that was meant to bring freedom ended up enslaving them. You could say that they exchanged trying to make bricks without straw to trying to be righteous without grace.

The fear of losing their independence as a nation, of losing those various distinctive food laws and Sabbath recognition, etc, which marked them out as God's people was so great that they ended up being enslaved to these very laws. As when studying something through a magnifying glass, what you focus on you get more of, and so if you focus on the law you become more legalistic. They lost sight of the purpose for which it was given in the first place. We can clearly see the outcome of this in the New Testament:

> Now then, why do you try to test God by putting on the necks of Gentiles a yoke that neither we nor our ancestors have been able to bear?
> (Acts 15:10)

We see this graphically in Matthew:

> Then Jesus said to the crowds and to his disciples: 'The teachers of the law and the Pharisees sit in Moses' seat. So you must be careful to do everything they tell you. But do not do what they do, for they do not practise what they preach. They tie up heavy, cumbersome loads and put them on other people's shoulders, but they themselves are not willing to lift a finger to move them.'
> (Matthew 23:1-4)

The word 'yoke' is not explicitly used, but we see a very clear description of a heavy burden. The law had become a yoke in itself, which the religious leaders were happy to impose on the people.

So often, we don't fully appreciate what we have or the situation we are in until things change, for better or for worse. Likewise, the Israelites could not see how the law had enslaved them until Jesus came, shedding new light and exposing what had happened. Only then could they wake up, understand why it was no longer working and finally realise that there was a better way. They did not know and could not know this before, which is why the explicit references to this are in the New Testament, with only prophetic suggestions in the Old. The apostles were adamant in their condemnation of the engrained way of thinking and worked hard to prevent it from entering the early Church.

The promise of release

We have clearly seen that a recurring theme in the Old Testament is the cycle of slavery and release.

Just as the book of Judges serves as a microcosm, the Exodus story of slavery and freedom through the Passover is repeatedly reflected in Israel's history, where they are enslaved and then liberated by God. A final solution to break this never-ending problem is provided when God intervenes in a radically new way through the incarnation of Jesus. Through His death and resurrection at the Passover as the Passover Lamb, reflecting the original Egyptian release so many centuries before, God puts in place the means to break the cycle.

When God redeems a situation, He always improves it beyond its original state.[68] Thus, in providing the solution for Israel's enslavement, He goes further and provides release for all humankind. Those verses we saw earlier in Isaiah announcing God's plan to remove the burden for the 'whole world' come good. He puts in place the means to set all humanity free from slavery. We see that a shift of emphasis has occurred, from predominantly nations, to religion being the oppressor, to finally the heart of the matter being addressed, which is our brokenness. It had become obvious that Israel and also humanity could not break this sequence of enslavement, no matter how hard they tried.

Rather than getting better, we as humanity seem, at least, not to be improving things but, in many ways, digging ourselves deeper into the mess we find ourselves in. Like Esau in Genesis, when Isaac heard his cry of pain, or the cry of the Israelites in Egypt, God hears the cry of all His children and promises that He would take them out from under the yoke.

Our lived experience as individuals and humanity shows that although Christ has set us free, we still get ourselves into trouble and continually need to be forgiven, redeemed and freed from what would enslave us. We don't have to look far to see the everyday example of the repetitive cycle from individuals frequently making the same decisions which get them into trouble, to nations who forget their history and repeat the mistakes of the past.

---

[68] For instance, Haggai 2:9 talks of the glory of the second temple being greater than the first.

In Leviticus 26:13, we read that God would remove the yoke so they could 'walk with heads held high'. Walking 'with heads held high' – what a promise! This is seen clearly in God promising to deal deeply with that enslaving attitude by replacing dead, cold hearts of stone with living hearts of flesh:

> I will give you a new heart and put a new spirit in you; I will remove from you your heart of stone and give you a heart of flesh.
> (Ezekiel 36:26)

My brother-in-law was a hospital theatre nurse, where he had to wear a lead apron to protect him from radiation that was used as part of the procedures he was helping with. The apron was very heavy and caused him to walk with a stoop and have back problems. It affected the way he walked. In many ways that is a good illustration of the yoke we are talking about here. The root cause of the problem was not the laws but the attitudes that enslaved.

Another notable passage is in Lamentations. It hints at this radical change of dealing with the root cause, which was not foreign domination or even the law, but sin. Sin can be incredibly inventive at taking just about anything and turning it around to harm. Written by Jeremiah, Lamentations says:

> My sins have been bound into a yoke;
> by his hands they were woven together.
> They have been hung on my neck,
> and the LORD has sapped my strength.
> (Lamentations 1:14)

We look forward to Jesus the Messiah finally releasing the captives.

Have you ever tried to unravel a tangled knot, and the more you try the worse it gets? We cannot undo the knot of what binds us ourselves! We are stuck in the middle of it, and the more we try the more of a mess we make. We need an outside agency to untie the knot. The Gordian knot in Greek mythology tells of a knot that was impossible to untie, saying that whoever could untie the knot would rule Asia. Alexander the Great solved this impossible problem and, rather than untying the knot, he took his sword and sliced right through it! Some things are impossible to untie, and the more we try the worse it gets. We need a different approach, which is what Christ did: He sliced right through it!

Jesus breaks the yoke

Jesus has led us out of slavery and continues to do so. Our confident hope is that on the last day, He will finally bring lasting freedom to all of creation, including us. That yoke of slavery will be fully and finally shattered to lie forgotten in the dust for evermore. Hallelujah! The critical thing has now become whether we will cry out to God, or continue to try to solve the problem in our own strength.

Unlike Pharaoh, Babylon, the religious leaders or even what the law had become, Jesus does not place an oppressive burden on His followers. Instead, He offers something radically different, with the weight of striving being replaced by an embrace of rest.

As we know, Jesus succumbs to the ultimate yoke of slavery in His death. He then rises again to release us from this ongoing repetitive story, redefining how release is found and reframing the entire narrative. Not just for Israel who were supposed to show the way to all humanity and be a 'light for the Gentiles' (Isaiah 49:6), but for all humanity, as this story repeats itself even today across the globe with tragic monotony. History often repeats itself, as we never seem to learn from it. And often, yesterday's good things become unhelpful today. Jesus radically lays an axe to the root of the problem. The Torah itself became a yoke; it was originally meant in a very good sense, but again, with humanity's amazing ability, became a yoke from which we needed to be freed.

We saw with Esau that restlessness broke his yoke; Isaiah takes a step further, talking about the yoke being broken or thrown off:

> In that day their burden will be lifted from your shoulders,
> their yoke from your neck;
> the yoke will be broken
> because you have grown so fat.
> (Isaiah 10:27)

In some translations, fat is translated as oil, and sometimes even as anointing oil, since the Hebrew word for fat, *shemen*, can mean fat or oil and is used in the context of anointing.[69] The KJV translates the last line as 'because of the anointing'. The anointing breaks the yoke and, of course, Jesus' gift of the Holy Spirit, that anointing which John talks about in his letter,[70] breaks the yoke. Not only

---

[69] See for example NKJV.
[70] 1 John 2:20, 27.

does the anointing break the yoke, but it also graciously places something entirely different on us that enables us to live in a new way. That new and entirely different thing is a loving relationship, experienced through the Holy Spirit, with our heavenly Father. We get fat, not in a 'prosperity gospel' way, but with God's blessing, so that the yoke simply breaks or even slides off as there is no room for it any longer in our lives. Sometimes, all we have to do is stop fixatedly preoccupying ourselves with the burdens we carry and instead focus on God's love, so they simply fall off. Returning to the magnifying glass analogy, when we focus on God's grace, we find a deeper sense of freedom in His love.

Take this forward to Jesus, where He said in Luke at the beginning of His ministry, after the wilderness temptations:

> The Spirit of the Lord is on me,
> because he has anointed me
> to proclaim good news to the poor.
> He has sent me to proclaim freedom for the prisoners
> and recovery of sight for the blind,
> to set the oppressed free,
> to proclaim the year of the Lord's favour.
> (Luke 4:18-19)

Jesus is anointed to break the yoke, and through His ministry He sends the Holy Spirit, breathing on the disciples in the upper room and, later, as wind and tongues of fire at Pentecost.[71] He breaks the yoke to set us

---

[71] See Acts 2.

free from sin, but also to release us into His kingdom. The father in the story of the prodigal broke the yoke of slavery and bondage off the son's neck and released him into the life of a son about his father's business.

Live by the yoke, die by the yoke

Let's change a well-known saying of Jesus to suit our purposes, from, 'If you live by the sword you will die by the sword,'[72] to, 'If you live by the yoke you will die by the yoke.' We read in 1 Samuel 6 that when the Philistines returned the captured Ark of the Covenant to Israel, they hitched the cart carrying the Ark to two cows that had just given birth and let them walk freely towards the border. Later, when David wanted to bring the Ark to Jerusalem, without thinking he did as the Philistines had done and also put it on a cart. The Ark of the Covenant represents and embodies the promise and presence of God. As the cart began its journey with its precious cargo, we read of tragic consequences as Uzzah reached out to steady the Ark, and was struck down and died.[73] David was shocked at what had happened, but later he remembered something about transporting the Ark of the Covenant.[74]

As king, he should have acquainted himself with the law on an annual basis and therefore ought to have known, as should his priests, that the Ark was specifically not to be carried on a cart, but on the shoulders of the Levitical clan of the Kohathites. This is expressly spelled out in Numbers 7:9. The Israelites, and in particular the

---

[72] See Matthew 26:52.
[73] 2 Samuel 6:6-7.
[74] 1 Chronicles 15:2.

leaders, naturally and without thinking, took on the cultural attitude and approach of the surrounding nations. They did this in so many ways, from appointing kings and taking multiple wives, to worship and carrying the things of God. We too, without thinking, can easily assimilate the thinking and approach of our culture to our faith, and have done this in regard to God's ways. We have taken the natural approach to what it is to be yoked and have not given it a second thought that we may have got it wrong.

The outcome of this way of thinking, as we see with David after the tragedy with Uzzah, is so often a sense of failure, low self-esteem, anger and resentment that begins with ourselves. It is not long until that eats away and the same feelings are displaced by anger and frustration which is transferred onto others. The religious leaders at the time of Jesus were transferring their own frustration and anger onto whoever would listen. We see this today, with some leaders doing the same; their expectations, sense of failure and frustration being transferred to their congregations, constantly encouraging them to do more, be more and give more, until both leaders and congregation are exhausted. That is surely of pharisaic roots, as we read in Matthew 23. I see much of this going on today, which is the same as the Jews struggled with all their days.

Job done

Paul talks in Galatians about the law fulfilling its purpose. The law, the Torah, was given as a teacher or 'guardian' (Galatians 3:24), to show that righteousness is gained not by works but by faith. Putting a yoke on someone does not set them free; it just highlights the need for freedom! Again, we can revisit the story of the prodigal son and see how his wrong thinking got him into trouble, being the cause of his bondage and servitude. It was also the trigger that made him realise that this course of action was not working. He had to get out of the confining situation he had got himself into, and it was the memory of home and his father's house that triggered his journey back, to find redemption for himself and, importantly, his thinking. It was through his father's embrace that he found freedom.

In fulfilling the requirements of the Law of Moses, Jesus takes us back to Abraham and the promises given to him. While the Law of Moses stood unfulfilled and broken, Israel was caught up in the never-ending cycle of trying to live up to it and failing, a bit like being trapped in a whirlpool. The promises made to Abram[75] stood open to be fulfilled, that his offspring would be blessed and be a blessing. Israel had clearly not fulfilled that, but in Jesus, it was finally fulfilled. We need to go back to Abraham, who predated Moses and the law, and look at God's promise and covenant with him, as it lays a foundation for what Jesus later did. In Galatians we read how the law had a specific purpose which has now been fulfilled.

It may be helpful to hear Paul's words in Galatians 3 and 4. The passages quoted below are quite long but worth reading as they develop and make very clear how all this fits together:

---

[75] Genesis 12:2-3 Abram and Abraham are the same person, named before and after a specific encounter with God.

> Christ redeemed us from the curse of the law by becoming a curse for us, for it is written: 'Cursed is everyone who is hung on a pole.' He redeemed us in order that the blessing given to Abraham might come to the Gentiles through Christ Jesus, so that by faith we might receive the promise of the Spirit. (Galatians 3:13-14)

Also:

> The promises were spoken to Abraham and to his seed. Scripture does not say 'and to seeds', meaning many people, but 'and to your seed', meaning one person, who is Christ. What I mean is this: the law, introduced 430 years later, does not set aside the covenant previously established by God and thus do away with the promise. For if the inheritance depends on the law, then it no longer depends on the promise; but God in his grace gave it to Abraham through a promise.
> Why, then, was the law given at all? It was added because of transgressions until the Seed to whom the promise referred had come. The law was given through angels and entrusted to a mediator. A mediator, however, implies more than one party; but God is one.
> Is the law, therefore, opposed to the promises of God? Absolutely not! For if a law had been given that could impart life, then righteousness would certainly have come by the law. But Scripture has locked up everything under the control of sin, so that what was promised, being given through faith in Jesus Christ, might be given to those who believe.

> Before the coming of this faith, we were held in custody under the law, locked up until the faith that was to come would be revealed. So the law was our guardian until Christ came that we might be justified by faith. Now that this faith has come, we are no longer under a guardian.
> (Galatians 3:16-25)

Finally:

> What I am saying is that as long as an heir is under age, he is no different from a slave, although he owns the whole estate. The heir is subject to guardians and trustees until the time set by his father. So also, when we were under age, we were in slavery under the elemental spiritual forces of the world. But when the set time had fully come, God sent his Son, born of a woman, born under the law, to redeem those under the law, that we might receive adoption to sonship. Because you are his sons, God sent the Spirit of his Son into our hearts, the Spirit who calls out, '*Abba*, Father.' So you are no longer a slave, but God's child; and since you are his child, God has made you also an heir.
> (Galatians 4:1-7)

Paul in these verses really labours the point about the law being fulfilled and our coming of age through the work of Christ Jesus!

It's breathtaking, as we move from the curse of the law and slavery to calling God, '*Abba*, Father'! Paul names it for what it is: the law became a curse. Not that it was wrong or inappropriate, but it had served its purpose; its job was done! He not only says the law is fulfilled, but he specifically takes us back before Moses, right back to Abram and his calling, when his faith was 'credited ... as righteousness' in Genesis 15:6. Right back to faith, and not works, defining how a relationship with God actually is meant to function.

God made a covenant with Abram, who later became Abraham. Abraham changed his very identity, and God altered His name to include God's name, 'ha', choosing to include Abraham, the one who acknowledged and believed, as part of His revelation of Himself. Often in Scripture God chooses to be known as the God of Abraham, Isaac and Jacob. Again, we see this idea of a close relationship coming into play.

Jesus takes the yoke of the cross of wood so we can take the Father's embrace, calling Him *Abba*. Jesus takes the curse of the law so the blessings of Abraham can be ours, not just the promise in Genesis 12 but also the covenant in Genesis 15. It is important to look at what this blessing and covenant is.

Abraham

The covenant found in Genesis 15 is important and needs to be considered as a basis for what comes later being fulfilled through Jesus.

Abram wanted assurance that God would fulfil His promises to him, and so God made a covenant with him:

> So the LORD said to him, 'Bring me a heifer, a goat and a ram, each three years old, along with a dove and a young pigeon.'

Abram brought all these to him, cut them in two and arranged the halves opposite each other; the birds, however, he did not cut in half. Then birds of prey came down on the carcasses, but Abram drove them away.

As the sun was setting, Abram fell into a deep sleep, and a thick and dreadful darkness came over him. Then the LORD said to him, 'Know for certain that for four hundred years your descendants will be strangers in a country not their own and that they will be enslaved and ill-treated there. But I will punish the nation they serve as slaves, and afterwards they will come out with great possessions. You, however, will go to your ancestors in peace and be buried at a good old age. In the fourth generation your descendants will come back here, for the sin of the Amorites has not yet reached its full measure.'

When the sun had set and darkness had fallen, a smoking brazier with a blazing torch appeared and passed between the pieces. On that day the LORD made a covenant with Abram.

(Genesis 15:9-18)

The covenant in Genesis 15 is different from the later Mosaic covenant. In the Mosaic covenant and other covenants at that time there was a requirement on both parties to fulfil their part, or penalties would follow. The Mosaic covenant had blessings for keeping and curses or penalties for breaking, as laid out at length in Deuteronomy 28. This seemed to be standard practice at that time, with records dating from the Hittites in Muri around the third millennium BC showing such a covenant being established. Animals would be severed and both parties would walk between the pieces as a sign that if either of them did not keep their side, then what happened to the animals would happen to them. We can see this in Jeremiah:

> Those who have violated my covenant and have not fulfilled the terms of the covenant they made before me, I will treat like the calf they cut in two and then walked between its pieces. The leaders of Judah and Jerusalem, the court officials, the priests and all the people of the land who walked between the pieces of the calf, I will deliver into the hands of their enemies who want to kill them. Their dead bodies will become food for the birds and the wild animals. (Jeremiah 34:18-20)

What is notable about the covenant made with Abram is that God alone in this theophany[76] goes between the pieces, thereby taking on Himself the penalty if either party fails to keep the terms of the covenant. If either side breaks the covenant, which of course God will not and cannot do, then He alone takes the consequences. The Lord literally cut a covenant, saying in effect that He would be like the severed animals if Abram did not fulfil the demands of the covenant.

This is important and relevant to our discussion, as the Sinai covenant has extensive, far-reaching penalties on the side of the Israelites. We see these penalties being played out time and time again because of Israel's repeated failure to keep the law. So much so that, as we have seen, many

---

[76] Theophany means manifestation or appearance of God.

lesser laws were written around the main law to protect it and prevent it from being broken.

In Deuteronomy 27 and 28, the contrast between blessings and curses is striking. There are sixty-six verses of curses and fourteen verses of blessings, giving a ratio of curses to blessings of five to one! Now, instead of this ratio of five to one, because of God's grace found in Christ there is no ratio at all, because God does not count our sins against us.[77] Do you remember 'the gift is not like the trespass'? God takes it all because the gift is not like the trespass, which is beyond comparison. The notion of scales, with sin on one side and our good deeds, or our faith, or indeed even Christ's sacrifice on the other side outweighing, or any other idea of ratios, is no longer applicable. This 'natural' way of considering, which I suggest all world faiths work on, is no longer valid as there are no scales, and there is no ratio.

Working on this basis of the ratio of blessings and curses, the idea of the law depicted as an animal yoke would be fitting with the two sides like a set of scales, two parties carrying the weight of obedience. Of course, the greater part, namely God, is able to keep His side flawlessly while we are not! The yoke of the law is one we cannot keep, but as Paul says in Galatians 3:19, it was designed precisely to make that abundantly clear.

Millennia after Abraham, Jesus exactly fulfilled the terms of that covenant by physically bearing the consequences in His own body of our failure to keep its terms. He did more than that: not only did He remove the negative aspect of slavery, but He also restored the

---

[77] 2 Corinthians 5:19.

positive aspect of intimate relationship, of which we had been robbed.

Imprinted

When studying psychological trauma, I learned of groundbreaking research called the Cherry Blossom Study.[78] In this study, mice were exposed to the scent of cherry blossom while simultaneously being given a mild electric shock. After a while, a sense of fear was imprinted in them so that they reacted negatively to the smell of cherry blossom, even when not exposed to electric charge. What is fascinating is that this fear response was evident in subsequent generations of mice, which exhibited the same reaction when exposed to the scent of cherry blossom. It appears that this fear response was imprinted at a genetic level.

This characteristic was first seen in combatants from the American Civil War when sons born of soldiers before they had fought, and particularly in those who had been in POW camps, had lower mortality rates than those born after.[79] The idea that trauma and adverse experiences can be passed down from generation to generation seems to carry scientific weight.

In Genesis 25:34 we read that 'Esau despised his birthright'. This strikes me as a remarkable retelling of the Adam and Eve story in the garden, who despised their

---

[78] www.news.emory.edu/stories/2013/12/smell_epigenetics_ressler/index.html; www.scientificamerican.com/article/fearful-memories-passed-down (accessed 16th May 2025).

[79] www.bbc.co.uk/future/article/20190326-what-is-epigenetics (accessed 16th May 2025).

birthright as sons and daughters of God, trading it for that piece of fruit. Here we have Esau trading his and his grandfather's birthright for a meal. Esau's attitude placed a yoke on his neck, and Adam and Eve's attitude placed a yoke on all our necks and imprinted something deep within the human soul that we see repeated over and over again. Abram in Genesis 12 recovered God's birthright to be a blessing and to bring life to all nations. In John 1:12 we read:

> Yet to all who did receive him, to those who believed in his name, he gave the right to become children of God.

Jesus knew and valued His birthright, His identity, not despising it but valuing it above all. The devil challenged this many times, including the time in the wilderness when he tempted Jesus, who was very hungry, by saying, 'If you are the Son of God, tell these stones to become bread' (Matthew 4:3). In this, His identity and birthright as the Son of God, which was spoken over Him at His baptism,[80] was being questioned and, again, for food! That same temptation, which had been successful on many occasions, failed this time, setting the scene for this wonderful new thing to happen. Jesus restores to us, in the new creation, the freedom of our birthright as sons and daughters of God, 'not of … human decision … but born of God' (John 1:13). We can clearly see this in the story of the prodigal who forgot and despised his birthright for

---

[80] Matthew 3:17.

food, even eating pigswill, and then in coming home was restored by the father's embrace.

Summary

The types of yokes we have looked at – despising our birthright, oppression of other nations or even the law itself and of our own sin – have been shattered by Jesus, and so we are now able to go back to an earlier promise and covenant which still stands.

God has fulfilled the requirements of the Mosaic covenant and law in Jesus' life. Through His death on the cross, Jesus has fulfilled the promise and covenant with Abram. This releases us from the oppressive yoke of performance-based religion to a new-found freedom. As children of God, this is our birthright, so rather than dismissing it for whatever reason, we should grasp it with both hands and live confidently in it.

Waymarker

Sit
Find somewhere quiet where you can relax and be undisturbed. This may be a favourite chair or a favourite walk.

Reflect
On your journey with this book so far, how has God made you aware that the old way of thinking is inadequate?

What does it feel like to find a new but ancient way of living, to leave the old performance way of faith and enter in to the new relationship of freedom through the Son of God who loved us and died for us?[81]

What have you been focusing on in your life: your failures or God's gracious love? Reflect on what it means to you that God willingly took the consequences of your brokenness, failure, shortcomings... everything that you don't like and despair of in yourself.

He planned this for you thousands of years ago. How does that make you feel?

Pray
Thank Jesus for not only taking your place but that God promised in ancient history to do this. Ask Him to lead you further into the life to come.

---

[81] Ephesians 5:2.

8
Rest in creation

He will cover you with his feathers,
and under his wings you will find refuge;
his faithfulness will be your shield and rampart.
Psalm 91:4

Sabbath rest

The command to rest is found in the fourth of the Ten Commandments, which is repeated in Exodus and Deuteronomy with interesting differences, particularly regarding the reasons for keeping the Sabbath. We are told in Exodus to rest because God rested. Rest from the very start was embedded in creation because even the Creator rested, making it a foundational principle:

> Remember the Sabbath day by keeping it holy. Six days you shall labour and do all your work, but the seventh day is a sabbath to the LORD your God. On it you shall not do any work, neither you, nor your son or daughter, nor your male or female servant, nor your animals, nor any foreigner residing in your towns. For in six days the LORD made the heavens and the earth, the sea, and all that is in them, but he

rested on the seventh day. Therefore the LORD blessed the Sabbath day and made it holy.
(Exodus 20:8-11)

In Deuteronomy the command is the same, but the reason given for rest is different. This time the emphasis is that we rest because we need to, we rest because we can and we rest because we have been set free.

> Observe the Sabbath day by keeping it holy, as the LORD your God has commanded you. Six days you shall labour and do all your work, but the seventh day is a sabbath to the LORD your God. On it you shall not do any work, neither you, nor your son or daughter, nor your male or female servant, nor your ox, your donkey or any of your animals, nor any foreigner residing in your towns, so that your male and female servants may rest, as you do. Remember that you were slaves in Egypt and that the LORD your God brought you out of there with a mighty hand and an outstretched arm. Therefore the LORD your God has commanded you to observe the Sabbath day.
> (Deuteronomy 5:12-15)

I love the idea that when a parent is trying to get an overtired child to sleep, they will often lie down with the child, encouraging the restless little one to settle. If you are a parent, you will probably have done this. God, so to speak, lies down with us, quiets our souls and says, 'It's OK.' We rest because we desperately need to; God rests not because He has to but because He knows we need to.

The Sabbath is the rest of God, which is reflected both in creation and in how creation is designed to function. A piece of art reflects the artist, with the artist's touches, strokes and personality being evident in their work, as we are told clearly in the first chapter of Romans.[82] Part of this is God's desire and plan for His creation to rest being woven into the very fabric of creation.

We see that this rest is not only for the people of God but also for the foreigners, slaves, animals and, by default, fields; it is for all. It is peculiar that we are so quick to return to that driven place of work, often lamenting that there are not enough hours in the day and repeating the phrase, 'I'm so tired,' as a badge of honour. It is even more peculiar that pastors are often the first to break this principle and the worst at being driven to work harder and longer, then feeling guilty if they are not continually at the end of their strength. Leadership is about modelling and leading into what is good, creating an environment for growth.

We rest because God has removed the yoke from us, enabling us to exercise our freedom and recognise what has been done. This can be too radical and countercultural, going against our need to perform, for us to comprehend. The Pharisee or lawyer in us just doesn't like it. But 'the gift is not like the trespass'…

Sabbath day in creation

I remember the well-known teacher John Stott saying at a conference in Edinburgh, 'If you want to find a principle

---

[82] Romans 1:20.

that is creational and not cultural, go back before the fall.'[83] Following his advice, we go back to Sabbath in creation and what it was meant to be at the very beginning, before it became fractured in our understanding by sin, and interpreted by the self-righteous religious leaders of whatever religion as a tool to enforce their own view.

We need to go right back to the first chapter in Genesis, when humankind's first day was a day of rest. God specifically ordained that Adam and Eve's first day was a Sabbath day of rest.[84] It is deeply significant that they worked from rest, not rested from work. Their very first day was not just resting and doing nothing, but discovering who they were. They had time to know and understand that he was Adam and she was Eve, son and daughter of God, created in God's image and likeness. They were given this earth to look after, but before they could do that, they needed to know who they were – their identity, their birthright – and to rest and be comfortable in that. In the opening chapters of Genesis, we read that by the seventh day creation was completed in its vast and glorious array:

> By the seventh day God had finished the work he had been doing; so on the seventh day he rested from all his work. Then God blessed the seventh

---

[83] Charlotte Chapel, Rose Street, Edinburgh. Late 1990s or early 2000s. Paraphrased.

[84] Genesis is ambiguous about the exact timing of Adam and Eve's appearance on the scene of creation. Genesis 1:27-28 suggests that God created both in the act of creation on the sixth day. The precise timing of what happened on day six is open to interpretation. I have decided to include both Adam and Eve on this sixth day.

day and made it holy, because on it he rested from
all the work of creating that he had done.
(Genesis 2:2-3)

God created the Sabbath and made it holy. Sin was not present in those days, so 'holy' cannot mean the absence of sin, but something else. Holy meant that it was set aside and dedicated to something specific, making it fit for the purpose it was created. Sabbath was holy because God rested and the day was specifically set aside for resting.

At Bible college, I was delighted to learn that Genesis can be seen as a missional book written into the culture of its day. Genesis seems to have been composed later than much of the contemporary literature – for instance, the Gilgamesh epic – and in writing into that culture and worldview, Genesis was correcting the belief that gods (plural) are violent and uncaring. Genesis describes a loving, caring and thoughtful God and, as such, in itself may be seen as a missional document revealing the true nature of God, as against a fearful culture based on appeasing angry gods. We have a vivid picture of God who rests and wants creation and all that is in it to rest, including Adam and Eve. As the final and integral part of creation, it is critical that they, more than any other, rest, as they hold the key and have been given stewardship and dominion. If they do not rest, how can creation rest?

There are eight elements to creation, the 'God said' moments:[85]

- When light was created

---

[85] Genesis 1:3-26.

- When waters were separated.
- When dry land appeared.
- When land produced vegetation.
- When lights in the sky separated day and night.
- When waters teemed with life and birds flew.
- When life appeared on the land.
- When God made humankind in His image.

John Crossan argues that the creation account is poetic in that the author was aware that he didn't know the 'how' of creation, but was describing the 'why'.[86] The poet fits eight elements of creation into six days, the sixth day being a Friday when humankind was created. It would seem that the writer carefully constructs this account to suggest that maybe humankind is not the crowning glory of creation, but that Sabbath is. Eight elements of creation are made to fit into six days with an obvious climax in mind. This puts a particular significance on day seven, the Sabbath, saying that creation was crowned, and still is, by the Sabbath. As Crossan points out, the Sabbath was the high point or apex of creation when the work was finished.

We need to reflect on the message of the first two chapters of Genesis, of Adam and Eve being made in the image of God and being commissioned to rule and be stewards of creation and of Sabbath. Humanity is created in the image and likeness of God, and next, that status is immediately shown as having dominion or rule over the

---

[86] John Crossan, *How to Read the Bible and Still be a Christian*, San Francisco, CA: Bravo, HarperCollins Publishers, 2016.

earth, as being part of what our divine image means. Finally, it is clear that God, whose image we bear, is the God of Sabbath rest. We are to rule the earth from and in that Sabbath rest of God, as that is a fundamental part of what it means to be human.

Sabbath, as we have read, has a clear purpose in Exodus, which is expanded slightly in Deuteronomy to emphasise that servants, livestock and working animals are to be included. During the Sabbath years every seven years, this principle broadens to even include the land. Rest is part of the worship of God as it is a demonstration and act of trust and faith. Trusting that God will supply your needs for one day of every week, taking time to stop and rest, then trusting God to supply your needs one year out of every seven, and then at Jubilee, pausing every forty-nine years, is a demonstration of active trust and worship.

Humanity's call to reign

In this Genesis passage, the Sabbath is of deep significance as it is the pinnacle of creation and the destiny of humankind and creation itself. The entire arc of Scripture leads to the magnificent vision of the New Jerusalem as part of the new creation, being the final, all-encompassing reign of God. In that wonderful final Sabbath rest to which our Sabbath points, we see why it is the culmination and fulfilment of creation. Tom Wright, in his book *Surprised by Hope*, comments that all of creation will be redeemed, and humankind, as part of this creation, will know and be included in this glorious setting free.[87] Creation will finally

---

[87] Tom Wright, *Surprised by Hope*, London: SPCK, 2007, p209.

know Sabbath rest, as we as humanity finally know this rest as well:

> I consider that our present sufferings are not worth comparing with the glory that will be revealed in us. For the creation waits in eager expectation for the children of God to be revealed. For the creation was subjected to frustration, not by its own choice, but by the will of the one who subjected it, in hope that the creation itself will be liberated from its bondage to decay and brought into the freedom and glory of the children of God.
> (Romans 8:18-21)

The Sabbath, then, as day, a year and as Jubilee, is a foretaste of this eventual reality for all creation in which we are included. In our self-centredness, we make ourselves the centre of the story, while in reality it is about the whole of creation being redeemed and resting – of which, of course, we are a part.

Humanity was created to steward and care for the earth, exercising dominion over creation from a place of rest, because true authority flows from rest, not striving. Jesus Christ has picked up and carried that yoke of creation rule that humanity put aside at the beginning and, taking it on Himself, invites us into it. However, we will not rule creation as our fallen nature thinks, but as our redeemed nature enables, which is in rest. Jesus is inviting us to take this yoke upon us and is calling us into this place of rulership. It is only in Him, who is seated above all, that we find our place, 'seated ... in the heavenly places', as Paul puts it in Ephesians (Ephesians 1:20; 2:6, ESV). We are invited into this place which has been open to us from creation but was soon closed when sin entered the scene. This call is great and is made possible through Jesus and the power of the Spirit.

The call of the prodigal son in the father's house to rule as he was originally born to do is huge, beyond the son's ability or comprehension, but in his father's love he was qualified to do exactly that. Our original calling to rule and reign is being restored in Jesus' invitation to take His yoke upon us.

Home

The true meaning of 'home' is something the prodigal son learned, and the older brother sadly had not by the time we left him standing in the field. The prodigal learned who he was and, more importantly, who the father was. As we know, he left his father's house hoping to find himself and establish his independence with an 'I know better' attitude. Like his older brother, he was in the father's house, but most certainly was not at home. Like the well-known saying, 'Home is where the heart is,' we see that their hearts were clearly not in the father's house. The younger son left but eventually came to his senses, realising that home was actually the place his heart was yearning for. He found out the hard way that the father's house was where he would be all that he was created to be, as his identity and purpose lay in relationship to his father.

When you take a step back and look at the bigger picture, this is the overarching theme of the biblical narrative. Adam and Eve were in the Father's house, Eden, but they were not truly at home. If they had been, the serpent's words would have fallen on deaf ears. Their leaving was necessary so they could come to their senses, recognise what had been lost and, in returning, receive the Father's embrace, finally finding their true home.

I think that God, in knowing the beginning from the end, knowing that the Sabbath was and is the culmination of creation, with complete understanding saw that Adam and Eve and so all humankind had to leave the garden to come back again. They had to leave so they could return and know that divine embrace and relationship as sons and daughters. We had to leave home to know where home truly is and will be for eternity. Our true self.

The first day of created living for humankind was a day of rest. Get that first step wrong and you will be stumbling the rest of the journey on the 'wrong foot' and will continue to be out of step all of life. We all need at some point in our lives to stop and learn what it is to start again on the correct footing; to know forgiveness, rest and a radical recalibration that is only found in Jesus' yoke of the Father's embrace. Nothing gets us on the correct footing except that embrace. We also need to know what it is to 'keep in step with the Spirit' (Galatians 5:25), as, after all, the anointing breaks the yoke, helping us again to find this place of rest. Jesus did this constantly in His ministry, not only because He had a deep relationship with His Father, but that we may also learn from His example.

Sabbath as mission

We saw in Matthew 11–12 that Jesus as rabbi unpacks and introduces a different understanding of Torah, of which a key part is the Sabbath and Sabbath rest. He combines the creational principle of Sabbath with His teaching and understanding of rest.

When I look around our world, I see humanity as a race and people as individuals desperately needing and seeking rest. It appears to me that everyone is seeking rest in one form or another. We are all looking to satisfy that deep need of rest which is inherent in us, as we are all inescapably part of creation. From the religious person trying so hard in so many ways to appease God, to the humanist who still seeks rest but in different ways, all trying so hard to please, gain, master and rule in whatever way they think best, so that they can rest.

The call of God to Sabbath rest is for all humanity, and we all desperately still need to hear it. Jesus' followers should know better than anyone what God's rest is and looks like, so that we can bring that good news to a restless world. If we do not know what it is to live in this rest, we cannot bring it to others, first in deed and then in word.

God calls us to be people of peace and so to be peacemakers. When we know a peace like this and are at peace within ourselves, then we truly have a message to bring; a message which communicates that creational depth of rest which is beyond words and which we will experience fully in the age to come. How our hearts yearn for that. It's a deep, multi-dimensional rest for our souls, for who I really am at my core, the *shalom* of God's peace in my true self. As God always improves on what was lost, we will experience in the new heaven and the new earth a rest far better than what was known and lost in Eden. All of creation deeply longs for this.

We yearn for deep intimacy with God, to open ourselves to the One who breathed life into us at creation in that profoundly close, life-giving moment. Even now, true life is found in this sacred exchange of God-breathed and God-embraced intimacy.

Life is still to be found in this God-breathing and God-embracing intimacy. In that wonderful moment, God breathed life into Adam and Eve, and breathing is still one of the vital signs of life, as we all breathe in and breathe out. We can hold our breath for a short period, but eventually we all need to breathe. God breathes His rest into us and He expects us to breathe out that rest. We breathe in God's forgiveness and so can breathe out forgiveness; we breathe in God's grace and so breathe out God's grace; we breathe in God's love and so breathe out God's love; and we breathe in God's peace so we can breathe out God's peace. We cannot be people of peace until we ourselves know that peace, not as a concept but as a reality of that God-breathed life.

We are called; our missional call is to be a people of rest, pointing to and inviting others into this rest, peace and fresh purpose for our lives, which Jesus offers and is still open to all. As I said before in talking of being people of rest, I am not meaning being inactive or passive, but of working and engaging in the world from a place of rest. Not driven out of a need to justify ourselves, but rather motivated from a sense of true self and seeking to bring that to others. We must know and embody that peace and then bring that peace to the world in ways that are understandable to those who don't yet know.

In Psalm 51, David asks God to forgive him, to wash him and to restore the joy of His salvation. He goes on to say, 'Then I will teach transgressors your ways' (Psalm 51:13). David knows that once the joy and peace of forgiveness, of intimacy with God, are a reality in his life, he has something to say and something to pass on. I see so many who are obviously not at peace, trying to bring peace – which they cannot, as it is still beyond them. They need to reset and get back on the right foot again!

The open secret is that an infinitely loving God actually seeks and desires intimacy with the human beings He created. Once we experience such intimacy or desire for this union, then only the intimate language of lovers describes what is going on – mystery, tenderness, singularity, specialness, nakedness, risk, ecstasy, incessant longing, which inevitably includes suffering. Our biggest secrets and desires are only revealed to others, and even discovered by ourselves, in the presence of love. We can be vulnerable, as we are entirely safe in the arms of love in the Father's embrace.

When the yoke that Jesus brings is worn, there is always peace and enriching of life as we have the opportunity to be larger people. Those who are too selfish or fearful to trust remain smaller than they need to be, as it is only when we are in such a tender place that God can safely reveal Himself to us. Those who are self-sufficient remain outsiders to the mystery of divine embrace, but we who are in Christ can know this rest, this deep rest not just for our bodies, but also for our very souls. We have something to say that surely everything and everyone longs to know and hear.

In Isaiah, God calls for chains to be loosed and the yoke untied. God Himself does this first but expects His people to follow suit:

> Is not this the kind of fasting I have chosen:
> to loose the chains of injustice
> and untie the cords of the yoke,
> to set the oppressed free
> and break every yoke?
> Is it not to share your food with the hungry
> and to provide the poor wanderer with shelter –
> when you see the naked, to clothe them,
> and not to turn away from your own flesh and blood?
> Then your light will break forth like the dawn,
> and your healing will quickly appear;
> then your righteousness will go before you,
> and the glory of the LORD will be your rear guard.
> Then you will call, and the LORD will answer;
> you will cry for help, and he will say: here am I.
>
> If you do away with the yoke of oppression,
> with the pointing finger and malicious talk,
> and if you spend yourselves on behalf of the hungry
> and satisfy the needs of the oppressed,
> then your light will rise in the darkness,
> and your night will become like the noonday.
> (Isaiah 58:6-10)

God sets us free from the yoke of slavery so we can, in turn, set others free. Jesus said, 'Freely you have received; freely give' (Matthew 10:8), and if we have breathed in God's peace, known it for ourselves, known His release and His yoke of embrace, then we are called to breathe out. Breathing out and living lives that set others free.

In today's world, we see so much suffering, which is clearly not as God intended. Creation is not at rest!

Creation is 'groaning', longing for liberation from bondage (Romans 8:19-22), waiting for us to take our place. This must include talking about the redemptive work of Christ but also, crucially, includes ministering in areas of justice, comfort, healing, trafficking, environment, work, debt, etc. The areas of need are many and cover every situation that dehumanises people, enslaving and imposing burdensome yokes. They cover all of creation, and so, whatever God has laid on your heart, wherever you see a lack of peace, this is your calling: to bring His presence, hope, peace and rest.[88]

Summary

We have seen that God's rest is for all creation and is something which will finally be fully realised in the new creation and also in our lives. As Jesus' followers who seek to live in obedience to Him now through the power of the Holy Spirit, we are also called to look forward, anticipating the final reality of God's rule on earth, which is this all-encompassing rest.

As we embrace Sabbath rest, we align ourselves with the rhythm of creation, stepping into the peace that God intended for all. We are called not only to embrace that rest and peace but to seek to lead others into it as well.

---

[88] Chris Wright. *The Mission of God's People*, Grand Rapids, MI: Zondervan Academic, 2010, is an excellent work to grasp the scope of this.

Waymarker

Sit
Find that place of rest where you can be undisturbed and have space and time to reflect and pray.

Reflect
Are you sitting comfortably? Not in the sense of physical position in a chair, but as a person loved by God? God came as a human being, which means it is good to be human. Are you comfortable in your humanity, your call as a child of God? Are you comfortable in being who you are?

Are there any areas which the Lord would lay on your heart to engage in?

Pray
Thank God for your humanity. Ask God if there is anything you need to come to terms with as a human being living out your life and call.

If God has laid a specific issue or people on your heart, take time to pray into that and what your response should be. If you sense a specific calling, you may need to pray further and talk it over with trusted friends.

9
A big picture

> The big picture doesn't just come from distance; it also comes from time.
> *Simon Sinek*[89]

A bigger picture

I am someone who likes to see the big picture, as then the smaller details make more sense. As a civil engineer working on large and complicated construction schemes, it was crucial to grasp the big picture to know how the individual elements of the project fitted in and to ensure that they would all line up with each other. There is no point in building a section of road or tunnel if it does not meet the next section, or you could end up getting two tunnels for the price of one!

Likewise, when you understand the big picture of Scripture, the smaller parts align more clearly, making errors in interpreting individual passages and taking them out of context less likely. We have gone way back to the beginning in Genesis and seen that rest is an integral part of God's creation, and in going forward, saw a revelation

---

[89] www.brainyquote.com/quotes/simon_sinek_418544 (accessed 4th April 2025).

of the new heaven and new earth where the ultimate rest of all creation and humanity are accomplished. The creation we live in today is not the final product of God's plan but is His work in progress.

In Jesus' teaching on His yoke of rest, we have touched on very deep things that reveal something of the underlying principles and overarching story of creation.

There are many wonderful themes that run through Scripture which bring an amazing richness. I suggest that there are two strands, or principles, which we will consider in this chapter that run through the Bible from start to finish, and which will help us understand the big narrative into which the smaller narratives fit.

Underlying principle

In that wonderful hymn in Philippians 2:6-11 about Jesus humbling Himself, becoming a servant and then being raised to the highest place, we see the turning point of the passage in verses 8 and 9 where we read:

> And being found in appearance as a man,
> he humbled himself
> by becoming obedient to death –
> even death on a cross!
>
> Therefore God exalted him to the highest place
> and gave him the name that is above every name.
> (Philippians 2:8-9)

The pivot point of all of creation's story is the humbling of Christ Jesus to the point of death so that God could exalt Him to the highest place, and in this we see an underlying principle of humility and sacrifice.

Heaven is a place of perfect love where the Father glorifies the Son, the Son glorifies the Father and the Spirit glorifies each one! Heaven is a place where we might say a different language is spoken, a language of humility, preferring one another, living lives of giving and sacrifice, engaging in uncompromised worship and casting our crowns before the throne of God. This principle of humility and sacrifice runs throughout history, starting with God's very act of creation, where He formed the world in such a way that allows humanity to reject Him. We know, of course, that Adam and Eve chose to reject God's counsel, yet God immediately intervened, covering their nakedness through the sacrifice of an animal. From creation to the new creation, this principle of humility and sacrifice shapes history, with the cross standing at its centre and turning point.

It was the tree of the knowledge of good and evil that was humanity's downfall and caused that change in our understanding of the principles or that language of heaven. We came to think it was about intellect, knowledge, power, works; about me and about what I can do. We lost the language of heaven, which Jesus came to restore, as only He is a native speaker and so able to teach us again. The gifts and fruit that the Holy Spirit gives us are words of this language.

We can trace this through Abraham, who approached God and received the promise by faith. In Psalm 51:17 we read, 'My sacrifice, O God, is a broken spirit; a broken and contrite heart you, God, will not despise.' Jesus talked much about this, and in the story of the prodigal son brought it into sharp focus with the qualification for the son to be accepted not having anything to do with strength or works, but the attitude with which he came: humility and brokenness.

God's intention is not to grind us into dust, making us feel wretched and of no value, but is quite the opposite. He wants to restore us to who He made us to be and who we really are. He formed us from dust, breathing life into us in the first place, so why would He want to undo the work that He has done and called 'very good' (Genesis 1:31)?

Later, during the intertestamental period and in Jesus' day, faith took on the characteristic of seeking righteousness through strict legalism and self-effort, an approach which we have seen simply did not work. We come in weakness and emptiness, with empty hands, open minds and humble hearts; 'a broken spirit; a broken and contrite heart you, God, will not despise'. This is part of what Jesus was saying in Matthew 11 when talking of His yoke; His rabbi's yoke was His teaching about how to come to God, how to be accepted by God and how to know God's rest; not in works, intellect or crushing religious observance but in childlike trust, humility and simple acceptance.

Many of us need to have our minds renewed in how we think and respond to grace. We know we need to come in humble acceptance, but old habits are deeply engrained and call us back to trying to live out our life of faith by works! It is a glaring contradiction, but is one that has been around for a very long time, which is why Paul tells us:

> So then, just as you received Christ Jesus as Lord, continue to live your lives in him, rooted and built

up in him, strengthened in the faith as you were taught, and overflowing with thankfulness.
(Colossians 2:6-7)

We start this life of faith in the acceptance of grace, but so quickly think when we trip up that we need to get ourselves sorted out before we come back to God, that we need to be in a better place before we come, and we try to do that in so many ways. In reality, we don't and can't come to God 'clean and sorted'; we come empty and broken and He cleans and sorts us. The very act of trying to be better and acceptable before we come is what can push us away. It's not that God cannot work in us but that we will not let him,[90] and of course, He has given us that free will. Again, as we read in Psalm 51, we must come to Him aware that He makes us whole.

The Jews were trying so hard to be on 'the inside' with God, as the religious leaders thought they had a special connection to Him. Yet by this very thinking they ended up on the outside. Jesus was very clear, saying that the tax collectors and sinners were the ones who found themselves inside the kingdom of heaven long before the ones who were trying so hard in their own strength.

We can try in so many ways to be on the inside with God, trying to be a good Christian, being moral and keeping what we perceive are the rules and expectations. We see this in our own Christian faith and we also see this in other faiths – all those washings, regular prayers and sacrifices of all kinds. We think this gets us closer to God, but it is based on the premise that it's all about us, what

---

[90] Isaiah 59:1-2.

we do and our terms, which in reality drive us further away. The prodigal son came in brokenness and was immediately brought into the father's house while the older son remained in the fields.

For humanity to rule well for the glory of God and the good of creation, we must learn this deepest of all lessons – that we rule and reign as we are created to do when we come from an attitude of humility and service. God created us with intellect, strength, gifts and abilities, all of which we must use, but in the God-given way of sacrificial service and not as a means of achieving power, status, independence and self-rule. In learning this and being filled with the Spirit, we are being prepared for that final time when we will reign with Him and will be equipped to do so as we will have learned that language of heaven.

The underlying principle of creation is sacrifice and humility, and in that attitude, God raised Christ to the highest place to establish the new creation. In the same way we are encouraged to do the same in the verses preceding the hymn in Philippians,[91] with the promise that, if we are united with Christ, God will raise us up with Christ. It is from this place that we will reign, and it is this reign of humble rest that creation is waiting for.

The overarching story

I have already covered this in some detail in the last chapter, but I will briefly summarise to refresh our memories. The father let the son have his inheritance and allowed him to leave, in the hope that one day he would come to his senses and return home. He, as a good parent,

---

[91] Philippians 2:1-5.

would most certainly have felt deeply, and been hurt by the distance between him and his sons. The father kept looking eagerly, waiting to see his boy returning in the distance. When the son eventually came home, he was welcomed not as a servant but as a son and, finally, he was at home in the father's house. Although he was in his father's house before he left, he was not at home.

Likewise, God was not taken by surprise when Adam and Eve ate the fruit from that tree and as a result had to leave the garden. They were in the Father's house but certainly not at home, or they would not have listened to the serpent. God let them go in the hope that one day humankind would come back – as time moved on, all of humanity is now involved in that original deed in the garden. He even sent His Son to help us find our way home, for in returning we would finally be 'home' in the Father's house, something we never were before.

In Jewish tradition, repentance and returning are closely linked in the Hebrew word *teshuvah*.[92] The idea of repentance in Jewish thought is a return to the path of righteousness, with sin understood as going astray. The prophet Hosea echoes this idea in his words:

> Return, Israel, to the LORD your God.
> Your sins have been your downfall!
> Take words with you
> and return to the LORD.
> (Hosea 14:1-2)

---

[92] www.myjewishlearning.com/article/repentance (accessed 4th March 2025).

Just as the younger son in the parable returned to his father, returning to God is deeply connected to repentance. This resonates with this overarching story I have described.

The eternal way of things

Taking the underlying principle and overarching story and placing it within the parable of the prodigal, we see the father longing for the son's return. God patiently calls and leads humanity back to Himself; this is why the old covenant, though glorious, was only temporary, pointing us towards the surpassing glory of the eternal embrace in the new covenant.

Paul in 2 Corinthians compares the new covenant with the old covenant or ministry, engraved in stone, referring to the Mosaic Law and the Ten Commandments, and how it came with glory which was temporary, as it faded. He asks a rhetorical question: how much more glorious is the ministry that brings righteousness compared to the one that brought condemnation?

> Now if the ministry that brought death, which was engraved in letters on stone, came with glory, so that the Israelites could not look steadily at the face of Moses because of its glory, transitory though it was, will not the ministry of the Spirit be even more glorious? If the ministry that brought condemnation was glorious, how much more glorious is the ministry that brings righteousness! For what was glorious has no glory now in comparison with the surpassing glory. And if what

> was transitory came with glory, how much greater
> is the glory of that which lasts!
> (2 Corinthians 3:7-11)

If the glory of that which was passing faded away, how much more glorious will be the glory of that which lasts? The Mosaic Law was temporary, with a set purpose to accomplish, which it did. The temporary has been replaced with something infinitely better in at least two ways; first because it achieves something that the temporary could never do, and second because it is permanent. It is the final, complete and eternal way of things.

The Law and the Prophets were a necessary interval before the final and permanent would come, similar to roadworks being necessary when building a motorway. They are not the final way of things, but a necessary temporary stage, pointing to something better that is coming. As the inconvenience of the roadworks continues, we increasingly look forward to and hope for the final result! In Christ, this better thing has come and is the permanent way of things from now on. The Father's embrace, this loving, intimate relationship with the Trinity through the work of Jesus Christ, is the eternal permanent way of things. It was and is and ever will be the nature of the divine Trinity and so will be the everlasting way of things in the new creation. What we have been describing and talking about in this book is much more than a nice idea or an encouraging spiritual exercise; it is the eternal way of things, the reality behind everything, absolutely everything! It is a wise person who sees this and begins to align themselves with eternity.

Paul calls us to be bold in the freedom found in Christ through the Spirit.[93] This is not something to approach cautiously but something to grasp with both hands and live out boldly. The prodigal son on returning did not push his dad away saying, 'I'll think about this. I'm not sure if this is something I can trust or even deserve!' He allowed himself to be embraced, kissed, robed with his father's best robe and fitted with new sandals. He fully accepted and did not question or hold back in any way. Any hesitation had already been fully dealt with. He knew he was not worthy, but his worthiness or lack of it was not the issue; it was the father's love and grace.

How dishonouring it would have been to reject the father's love. Yet, is that what we do? We read about this love, about the embrace, about grace and yet, somehow, we doubt and hold back, preferring our idea of how things should be, in contrast to the overwhelming evidence that love, grace and embrace is the eternal way of things. As we hold back from receiving this love, only one person is happy, and that is the older brother. Do we really want him to set the agenda for our lives and our happiness?

Radical repentance

In this journey we are making together I hope that a picture of God's grace and love for you is becoming clearer. However, it's not quite complete yet, as there is one more piece that needs to be added, to be grasped in greater depth, and that is what Jesus is saying in those verses we started with in Matthew: 'For my yoke is easy

---

[93] Galatians 5:1.

and my burden is light.'[94] I invite you to take one more step with me as we explore the Father's embrace and our understanding of what it looks like and how it affects us.

In Matthew 13, Jesus teaches about the kingdom of heaven in parables. There are two which many of us may know well: the parables of hidden treasure and a pearl:

> The kingdom of heaven is like treasure hidden in a field. When a man found it, he hid it again, and then in his joy went and sold all he had and bought that field.
> Again, the kingdom of heaven is like a merchant looking for fine pearls. When he found one of great value, he went away and sold everything he had and bought it.
> (Matthew 13:44-46)

The traditional understanding of these parables is that the kingdom of heaven is represented by the treasure and the pearl, which require us to sell or let go of everything in order to obtain them. That is what the prodigal son had to do in returning home. He had to swallow his pride and let go of everything to come home.

I agree with that interpretation; however, I think that another way of looking at these two little parables is from the father's point of view where he, too, gave up everything to accept his son back home. From an Eastern cultural context, which is based on an honour and shame orientation, the father allowed himself to be shamed and, in reality, gave up more than his son to be able to receive

---

[94] Matthew 11:30.

him home.⁹⁵ In light of the journey we have been on, without dismissing the traditional view, I want to consider this second point of view to appreciate these words in a new way. Could it be that we are the pearl of great price? In both of these powerful word pictures, a search is strongly implied, followed by a transaction in which everything is given to obtain the treasure.

God is the One who seeks us out.⁹⁶ He always has, from the initial moments in the garden when Adam and Eve distanced themselves from Him, right through all of history up to this moment. God seeks you and me. He seeks us, He calls us and we respond. He sought us out, long before we responded to His call, and He made the transaction long before we replied. It is God who, in Christ, gave up everything to have for the treasure you and me. It is God who took us from being buried and in darkness and raised us up into His light.⁹⁷ It is God who cleans us, washing and restoring us to what we were created to be.

We are the pearl of great price!

In Luke 15, the lost sheep was embraced, the lost coin was held and the lost son was enfolded. In the same way, the pearl was passive in this parable and was held. If the pearl had any say in the matter, it was to allow itself to be held. The challenge for us is not to negotiate or work in any way

---

⁹⁵ For a fuller understanding of this see Bailey, *Poet & Peasant* and *Through Peasant Eyes*, p 158f and the academic work by David A DeSilva, *Honor, Patronage, Kinship, and Purity: Unlocking New Testament Culture*, Downers Grove, IL: IVP, 2022.
⁹⁶ Luke 19:10.
⁹⁷ For a parallel Old Testament image of this see Ezekiel 16:1-14.

for our redemption and restoration, but to let go and let God do the work. To allow ourselves to be embraced. If we are the ones doing the seeking and buying of this invaluable treasure, then it means we are the ones who have control of the story, setting the narrative. This is surely the wrong way around, as it is God who sets the story and our part is the choice of how we respond.

This pearl, along with the other pearls God is seeking, redeeming and restoring, form His 'crown of splendour' and 'royal diadem' held in His hand (Isaiah 62:3).[98] Together we are being formed into the people of God for His kingdom. In describing the New Jerusalem in Revelation,[99] we read that it is made of treasures of different kinds, including pearls. As pearls of great price, we have a unique place in His crown for the purpose of God's glory and are a part of the New Jerusalem, the city of God, in the new creation.

We are created to enjoy and be enjoyed by the Trinity, so why do we look at God through cautious eyes? Why do some of us think that God the Father is angry and Jesus shields us from His wrath? We need to repent from this view of God and change our thinking. Our repentance does not trigger God to love us, as He already does that, but instead opens us up to receive this love. He loves us, seeking and valuing us to an extent that we cannot begin to understand.

Our usual understanding of the word 'repentance' finds its roots in the Latin, *paenitentia*, meaning remorse and change of heart; penance. However, the Greek word

---

[98] See also Malachi 3:17.
[99] Revelation 21:18-21.

used for repentance in the New Testament is *metanoia*, which means a change of thinking. To repent is not to burden ourselves with guilt, striving to earn favour and forgiveness; instead, it is to change our thinking about how God sees us. This word *metanoia* suggests a radical shift from thinking one way about God and ourselves to thinking another. This is a radical reorientation.[100]

There is no evidence that God was immediately angry with humanity after the Fall. On the contrary, He immediately showed that His love was always seeking to restore and repair what had been broken. The attitude of the father to the prodigal son, as we have seen, illustrates this beautifully.

To fall in love with the Father, Son and Holy Spirit because God first loved me, and always has, brings such a profound sense of belonging and security. Finally, I know beyond doubt that I am fully accepted, embraced and loved. All my previous misconceptions about God crumble to dust. I can truly say I am a child of God, and that changes everything.

> My old self has been crucified with Christ. It is no longer I who live, but Christ lives in me. So I live in this earthly body by trusting in the Son of God, who loved me and gave himself for me.
> (Galatians 2:20, NLT)

With this in mind, we can now turn to the next chapters, where we will explore how this can practically transform our lives today.

---

[100] Peter Wilkes, *What God Believes About You*, Exeter: Onwards and Upwards Publishers, 2019, pp108, 124.

Summary

The overarching story of returning home and the underlying principle of love, humility and sacrifice have their roots and final, permanent outworking in the very nature of God. We know that 'Jesus Christ is the same yesterday and today and for ever' (Hebrews 13:8), and so in tracing this narrative of grace, we are following the arc of God's love and purpose for creation, for humanity and, yes, for you!

I hope your understanding of how God sees you and how you see yourself has changed. In our seeking, valuing and owning the treasure of the kingdom, it was first of all us who were sought, valued and kept. We are the treasure of the kingdom. We may need to give up everything we hold dear to us in order to obtain this, but we also realise that God gave up everything to hold what is dear to Him, to hold us.

It is amazing to reflect on the journey – we have come from first thinking about Jesus' yoke being easy and light to grasping that inherent in that invitation is God's valuation of us.

Waymarker

Sit
Find that place you are familiar with now, and relax and let your mind rest.

Reflect
As you relax, close your eyes and ask the Spirit to guide your thoughts. Picture the vast, swirling galaxies. Some of the images from the Hubble Telescope may help, so

Google them if you would like to. Now imagine yourself as the pearl of great price, tenderly held in the same hands that formed those stars, the hands of a God who calls you His own. The hands that were spread and pierced on the cross now tenderly hold you. We are told that we are 'engraved ... on the palms of [His] hands' (Isaiah 49:16).

Pray
Thank God in your own words and way for what this means for you.

10
Today!

> It isn't enough to talk about peace. One must believe
> in it. And it isn't enough to believe in it. One must
> work at it.
> *Eleanor Roosevelt*[101]

My goal has been to paint a picture of what Jesus' rest looks like and why we can trust ourselves to Him and His yoke and so enter that rest, not as an academic exercise but as a life-transforming encounter.

In the last chapter we considered that we are not the seekers who pay the cost of finding the pearl of great price, but rather the actual pearl itself. If this is true, then many of our preconceived ideas fall to the ground. We do not purchase the pearl, or complete the transaction, but rather God has already done it. Our part in the story is not one of active searching, but of being found. The lost sheep in the parable in Luke 15 allowed itself to be found and carried back home. It had no control of the situation it was in and the only response was to allow itself to be rescued, albeit no doubt with a lot of wriggling. Wonderfully we read that the shepherd rejoiced not just in reaching home but in

---

[101] www.brainyquote.com/quotes/eleanor_roosevelt_131302 (accessed 4th April 2025).

the very journey home itself with a wriggling, smelly sheep on his shoulders. What a powerful picture of how God sees us and rejoices in carrying us on our journey, as well as the arrival home.

God has completed the ultimate transaction to redeem us, yet, as we have seen, we often make faith transactional. We prefer to carry the burden of that exchange because it gives us a sense of control. But that never was our responsibility to bear. From the very beginning, we were not created to carry that weight, or yoke. Instead, our role in this divine transaction is simply to be found, surrendering and receiving His embrace.

By allowing ourselves to be embraced and added to God's crown of splendour for His glory, we step into a place of wonderful security. From this safe place, we can now consider what this truth means for our lives today.

The way we trust and surrender ourselves to His embrace will be unique to each of us, as everyone walks their own path of faith. I would never presume to dictate *how* you respond, but I encourage you *to* respond with confidence. You may have agreed with some of what you've read and struggled with other parts; that's OK. What truly matters is knowing that the Father's embrace is for you, finding Jesus' yoke in a fresh new way that is meaningful and life-giving for you.

It is for now

The life of faith is one of not just being hearers of God's Word but doers by putting it into practice.[102] We use high-sounding words but they are of no value unless acted on

---

[102] James 1:22.

and lived out, being earthed in our daily lives. Our worship on Sundays should make a difference to our lives on Monday; if it doesn't, then it is a waste of time and we may as well pack our bags and go home now! This idea we are looking at of Jesus' yoke of rest must make a difference in our lives today.

We read in Psalms 95:7-8, 'Today if … you … hear his voice, "Do not harden your hearts,"' which is repeated in Hebrews 3 and 4. In these chapters there is a lengthy discourse on unbelief in the hearts of the children of Israel that prevented that generation from entering the rest of the promised land. We read:

> Today, if you hear his voice,
> do not harden your hearts
> as you did in the rebellion,
> during the time of testing in the wilderness,
> where your ancestors tested and tried me,
> though for forty years they saw what I did.
> That is why I was angry with that generation;
> I said, 'Their hearts are always going astray,
> and they have not known my ways.'
> So I declared on oath in my anger,
> 'They shall never enter my rest.'
> (Hebrews 3:7-11, citing Psalm 95:7-11)

Hebrews 4 goes on to say that the promise of entering His rest still stands and expands on what we have covered before about creation, with the writer confirming that the rest, the Sabbath, was the culmination of creation. Importantly, that rest is still open to be known and entered into today:

> For if Joshua had given them rest, God would not have spoken later about another day. There remains, then, a Sabbath-rest for the people of God; for anyone who enters God's rest also rests from their works, just as God did from his. Let us, therefore, make every effort to enter that rest, so that no one will perish by following their example of disobedience.
> (Hebrews 4:8-11)

In each of the days of creation there was evening, except for the Sabbath, when there is no mention of evening. William Barclay in his commentary on Hebrews points out that as the sun did not set on that first Sabbath day, it is therefore still day and that the Sabbath rest is still available, as it is still *today*.[103] It is not something to be put off or an opportunity that has been missed.

Despite God's promises, Israel never fully entered His rest. Hebrews reminds us that this rest remains open for the people of God, which includes us, as those who trust in Christ today. Those words in Hebrews, 'Today, if you hear his voice, do not harden your hearts,' tell us not to put on our armour, getting defensive, trying to justify ourselves and staying in our safety zone. This all adds up to the same thing, meaning that we close down and stay precisely where we are. It is in the context of this rest that Hebrews says:

> For the word of God is alive and active. Sharper than any double-edged sword, it penetrates even to

---

[103] William Barclay, *The Daily Study Bible Series: The Letter to the Hebrews*, Philadelphia, PA: Westminster Press, 1976, p 36.

> dividing soul and spirit, joints and marrow; it judges the thoughts and attitudes of the heart.
> (Hebrews 4:12)

This rest is still to be found, which can mean that there is a work to be done in our hearts so that we can accept it and enter into it.

Joshua, the one who was to lead Israel into the Promised Land of rest, was challenged by God at the very beginning of his leadership to be 'strong and courageous' (Joshua 1:7-9). We automatically think that was to do with the battles that lay ahead in overpowering the giants in the land, but a careful look at the passage indicates otherwise. He was to be strong and courageous in not allowing the word of Moses to depart from his mouth, meditating on it 'day and night'. If he was to know the power to enter the promised rest and lead others into it, he had to let the word challenge him deeply, reflecting on it and letting it divide spirit and soul.

In finding rest, God's rest and peace, we often have to look at areas in our own lives which we would rather avoid. We need to find strength and grace to conquer these difficult areas. To find rest first in ourselves, by finding rest in God and in doing this hard internal work, we will be able to lead others to this rest as well. The giants in the land out there are nothing compared to the giants in our own lives, and once we can conquer our own giants, then the others can be relatively straightforward! This internal work can often bring us to the point of brokenness, the realisation that we need help, so we drop all pretences and trust Him.

Hearing God's voice can be overwhelming, and many of us instinctively try to drown it out with activity rather than allowing it to deeply challenge us. Hebrews specifically acknowledges this struggle when God begins His work in us. Often, we feel unworthy or ashamed as He refines us, but Scripture directly addresses this just a few verses after describing His Word as a sharp, 'two-edged sword' (Hebrews 4:12, ESV). It reassures us:

> For we do not have a high priest who is unable to feel sympathy for our weaknesses, but we have one who has been tempted in every way, just as we are – yet he did not sin. Let us then approach God's throne of grace with confidence, so that we may receive mercy and find grace to help us in our time of need.
> (Hebrews 4:15-16)

Our time of need is when we feel so broken and bad about ourselves that we can lose hope, which is precisely when God commands us to come to Him! When we have no confidence in ourselves, we are told to come with confidence in Him.

Think of how the prodigal son felt in returning to his father and how that wonderful story played out. The son was broken, but the father was yearning for him to return. We, in our heads, know how the story goes, but when it is we who are the returning child, our hearts may not be so confident, which is exactly why we are given this verse! It is a dramatic putting-off of one yoke and taking-on of another, first for ourselves and then, because we have experienced it personally, for others as well:

> Therefore, brothers and sisters, since we have confidence to enter the Most Holy Place by the blood of Jesus, by a new and living way opened for us through the curtain, that is, his body, and since we have a great priest over the house of God, let us draw near to God with a sincere heart and with the full assurance that faith brings, having our hearts sprinkled to cleanse us from a guilty conscience and having our bodies washed with pure water. Let us hold unswervingly to the hope we profess, for he who promised is faithful.
> (Hebrews 10:19-23)

Again, we see that underlying principle at work of humility and vulnerability.

Breaking the yoke

Isaiah 58 calls us to join with the work of God in breaking the yoke:

> Is not this the kind of fasting I have chosen:
> to loose the chains of injustice
> and untie the cords of the yoke,
> to set the oppressed free
> and break every yoke?
> (Isaiah 58:6)

God calls us to break every yoke, yet religion, regardless of its form, often does the opposite, adding burdens instead of lifting them. We do not break yokes by simply increasing the burdens or replacing them with new ones that feel different but still weigh us down, much like the overused phrase, 'Not working harder but smarter.' It may seem like a shift, but in reality it is no different.

Scripture teaches that the gift is different from the trespass, meaning the solution must also be different from the problem. A new kind of yoke and a transformed attitude are required. In Isaiah 58, the oppressive yoke of legalism, bondage and slavery is not merely adjusted but completely replaced with the yoke of grace. We are not meant to trade one burden for another; we are called to break and shatter the yoke that holds us captive, for we can only carry one yoke at a time. Let it be the yoke of grace.

We cannot carry two yokes, we cannot serve two masters, but so often we get confused. We embrace grace and forgiveness when things get too much for us, and then, as they get better, we seem to go back to trying to earn our keep. We can only carry one yoke, our shoulders are not big enough for two, and the yoke of the innocence of Eden is gone, lost for ever to the tree of the knowledge of good and evil. We need to reach out for a different yoke which is, as we have seen, the embrace of life found only in Jesus. The yoke we seek today cannot be based on information, knowledge or performance, but must be one of a different sort. God wants us to return to a simple and childlike relationship, but it can never again be naïve. The innocence of childhood should know what it is to have that relational embrace of a loving parent for a son or daughter, and to feel completely comfortable in it.[104] We are challenged that:

---

[104] I recognise that sadly this is not always the case, and tragically this is not the experience of many children. God's design was that family

> It is for freedom that Christ has set us free. Stand firm, then, and do not let yourselves be burdened again by a yoke of slavery.
> (Galatians 5:1)

This rest will be finally and completely fulfilled in the age to come, but we are called to live lives leaning into the future now. The fruit of the Spirit in Galatians 5:22-23 is the life of the age to come working out in our lives in the present. The anointing breaks the yoke and the Holy Spirit's empowering presence in our lives brings the life of the age to come to us now.

Summary

We are encouraged not to put off or make excuses to respond to God's call for us to rest and trust Him. So often the reasons for not responding are not external ones but can be found in our hearts, which is one reason why God's word is sharp and brings to light those things we would hide. However, we are strongly told that there is help and strength to be found in this inward journey we are called to make, and that we can approach God with confidence through Christ.

Waymarker

Sit
Find that place which you are now familiar with and relax, asking God to speak to you

---

should be a safe place, but sin has robbed so many of that. If this is your experience and it is unresolved, then I encourage you to seek help. Please see 'A loving embrace for all' in the appendix.

Reflect

Are there any places in your heart that you are keeping from God? Are there any places you are ashamed of and where you need to feel God's touch? Are there places which are cold or even feel dead inside, and again you need God to touch and bring His resurrection life?

For some, these questions can be very painful, raising difficult memories and emotions. If this is the case for you, please make a point of speaking to someone you trust. It may be a friend or a professional counsellor. If things have been stirred up, then maybe God has brought you to this place so you can address them. I cannot stress strongly enough that you must not try to carry this alone.

Pray

Give these thoughts and feelings to God and ask Him for His help. He is not shocked or put off by anything you may say or feel.

11
Practical rest

> Rest time is not waste time. It is economy to gather fresh strength.
> *Charles Spurgeon*[105]

Our faith must be able to work in practice, otherwise it is academic theory. So often we can think we are exercising practical faith but actually it is just a mental exercise we are engaging in. Understanding the concept and theory is completely different from putting it into practice.

Four-dimensional rest

God's call to rest can be practically worked out in at least four dimensions, reflecting those that Jesus taught when He instructed on what was important:

> Love the Lord your God with all your heart and with all your soul and with all your mind and with all your strength.
> (Mark 12:30)

---

[105] www.joshkary.com/rest-time-is-not-waste-time (accessed 4th April 2025).

I am sure there are many other applications, but for now we can look at these four areas for practical outworking, namely heart, soul, mind and strength.

Before we unpack this, let's look at the gift of peace, God's all-encompassing *shalom* which Jesus promises, as this influences all these other aspects. Jesus said:

> Peace I leave with you; my peace I give you. I do not give to you as the world gives. Do not let your hearts be troubled and do not be afraid.
> (John 14:27)

This peace is not just an abstract concept but a tangible reality we can build our lives upon. When Jesus spoke of it, He also affirmed the Father's love for us, His own victory over the world, the call to be unafraid and the coming of the Holy Spirit to guide us. He then concluded with the powerful invitation, 'Rise, let us go from here' (John 14:31, ESV).

This section of John's Gospel begins with darkness: 'And it was night' (John 13:30), and Peter's confusion, as he misinterprets Jesus' intentions. Yet it ends with certainty. John moves from uncertainty to clarity, illustrating that this certainty is the foundation upon which our faith must be built. This is where we begin, knowing we are loved, living in peace and empowered by the One who has overcome. That is a yoke worth carrying, one that is deeply practical and, when embraced, truly transforms our lives.

A big part of this peace is to know we are forgiven, and in being forgiven we can forgive. We can forgive ourselves, others and even this broken world in which we live. Jesus' rest and His peace is a gift and a birthright of those who believe, but sadly there are so many who do not know the reality of Jesus' peace in their lives.

If you have lost His peace, I encourage you to reflect on where it slipped away. As Jesus is the one who gives us His peace, losing it often signals a loss of closeness with Him, His presence and His embrace. Stop and ask the Holy Spirit to guide you as to where, when and how you lost it, then speak to Him about it, knowing with confidence that you will be forgiven.

How do we live?

Here are the four areas with my thoughts on how these could be put into practice. There will be others, but hopefully these may get you thinking. I have placed opportunities to stop and reflect after each of the four areas and I suggest that if, when reading, a particular aspect stands out for you, that you take the opportunity to pause and engage with the Waymarker pause. Alternatively, you could wait until the end and stop to reflect then.

1. Heart
Emotional attachment

Sue Gerhardt in her book, *Why Love Matters*, talks about younger children's emotional development and attachment.[106] This relates to how well a young child is 'attached' to their parent and accordingly their degree of self-security. A well-attached child is secure and exhibits a

---

[106] Sue Gerhardt, *Why Love Matters*, Abingdon: Routledge, 2008, pp 88, 98, 105, 125, 169.

calmer response when the parent leaves and returns. This carries on into later life where a well-attached child copes much better with life's stresses and, among other things, will live longer, do better in life and, surprisingly, is less likely to end up in prison. She emphasises that hugs are a major part of this. Hugs enable the child to know and experience what a normal, settled emotional state feels and looks like. A young child is unable to calm their own emotions as a matter of simple development. There's nothing wrong with the child; they just need to experience a calm emotional state, so they know how to return to it and learn the tools to get there. A hug and an embrace are essential. We all know how an embrace at the right time helps us; we have seen it many times in others and, hopefully, experienced it for ourselves.

The embrace which Jesus talks about as His yoke is a helpful way to understand how God teaches us, through loving acceptance, and matures us for life and ministry. Again, think of the prodigal being embraced by his father, which is much more eloquent and meaningful than any number of words.

There are many verses in the Psalms where the psalmist talks of being under the shadow of His wings, knowing God's steadfast love and finding refuge.[107] This is a wonderful example of what it is to know and live in God's embrace, under His wings. This is the loving embrace of a caring parent which brings rest and calms our hearts. With a natural parent, we cannot remain permanently in this place, but with our heavenly Father, we most certainly can. Imagine living your whole life in this embrace, from

---

[107] For example, Psalms 36:7; 57:1.

when you wake in the morning until sleep calls, and even when asleep and you are unaware, the embrace never ceases! Is this what praying 'without ceasing' is?[108]

Many of us may not have had the easiest or most peaceful childhoods, and our lives may have been filled with struggles. In the book of 1 Chronicles we read about a man named Jabez, whose name literally means 'sorrow' or 'trouble'. His life and family history were marked by hardship. While he couldn't change his past, Jabez sought to change his future and that of his children and those around him. So he prayed:

> And Jabez called on the God of Israel, saying, 'Oh, that You would bless me indeed, and enlarge my territory, that Your hand would be with me, and that You would keep me from evil, that I may not cause pain!' So God granted him what he requested.
> (1 Chronicles 4:10, NKJV)

This story is a great encouragement, showing us a practical example of what God can and wants to do in our lives. Just as Jabez turned to God to change his circumstances, we, too, can take steps to find healing and help for ourselves. By doing so, we can also make a positive impact on the future and on those around us, turning difficult situations into opportunities for growth and blessing.

Waymarker pause
Maybe you would like to stop right now and sit, allowing yourself to be embraced by God. Does any of what you

---

[108] 1 Thessalonians 5:17, ESV.

have just read affect you in ways you did not expect? What do you want to do about this?

2. Soul
Breathe!

The Greek word for soul is *psuché*, meaning breath or soul. It is used in the context of 'the vital breath, breath of life, or the human soul'. Closely related is the word *psyxé*, meaning to breathe, or to blow. This is the root of the English word 'psyche', as in psychology. The soul or psyche is a person's distinct identity. This corresponds exactly to the Old Testament word *nephesh*, again meaning soul.[109] From this it is reasonable to think that the soul is the direct result of God breathing or blowing His gift of life. For those who have had the privilege of witnessing a birth, it is a miraculous moment of wonder when that first breath is taken.

To be able to sit and allow God to breathe into us again is a vital part of Christian faith. Following the Reformation, parts of the Protestant Church became suspicious of contemplation and reflective practice and, in some places, shunned it. Thankfully it is being rediscovered.

I have found soul rest in simply sitting with Jesus; not actively praying or trying to do anything, but just 'being' in His presence. If this is difficult for you, then a walk in nature can be helpful. I find that sometimes when I start, like Elijah, my emotions can be all over the place,[110] but as

---

[109] Strong's Lexicon accessed through BibleHub.com. www.biblehub.com/hebrew/5315.htm (accessed 5th April 2025).
[110] 1 Kings 19. Elijah was traumatised and exhausted, with his emotions being in tumult. We read that before he heard God in a

I walk or sit, I begin to hear birdsong, wind in the trees or my own breath, and then I know I have quieted my soul, and again like, Elijah start to hear the 'still small voice' (1 Kings 19:12, NKJV).

Being whole
An integer is a whole number with no divisions or fractions, which is where we get the word 'integrity' from. Psalm 51:6 talks of God: 'Surely you desire integrity in the inner self' (CSB). The idea is clear that there should be no fractions or separate areas in our lives but a consistency of truthfulness, integrity and wholeheartedness in the innermost being. Who David the psalmist is on the surface is who he is in the innermost being. No conflict, hypocrisy or angst. This is what being 'wholehearted' means.

David prays in this psalm that when God has restored 'the joy of [His] salvation' (v12) then he will 'teach transgressors [God's] ways' (v13), as he has something now to share. The joy of salvation is closely linked to the idea of integrity and gives David a strong place to live from, similar to what we were previously talking about of God doing a deep work in us.

This goes back to Paul saying in Colossians that God has reconciled 'to himself all things' through Christ (Colossians 1:20), and also Jesus' words in John 14:23, that the Father and Son have made their home in us. Integrity, no conflict or divisions in our lives, is what the idea of reconciliation means – reconciled to who I am. That does

---

whisper there was a strong wind, an earthquake and a fire. Sometimes I find this reflects my strong emotions that need to be worked through before I can hear that 'gentle whisper' of God.

not mean I am sinless or without fault – that will come as God does His work – but at the moment, I am called simply to rest in God who knows all about me, who has forgiven me, who is still at work in me by the power of His Spirit, so I can rest in the arms of the Father.

The father embraced all that the son was on his return: the filth, the smell, the journey and the rejection. The father embraced it all. Our heavenly Father embraces all that we are: our innermost thoughts, rebellion, sin, our journey away from Him, the depths of sin we may have descended to and also the heights of praise. All are embraced and laid to rest. So we, too, can rest in this living embrace.

Waymarker pause
Breathe.[111] It may feel strange to begin with, but as you breathe, take note of feelings which may bubble up. Don't try to analyse them but simply trust that God knows all about them, and through the work of the cross has reconciled Himself to them so that you can as well. There may be things that still challenge you from the previous chapter, but for now, trust that God knows all about them. Simply give them back to God in prayer.

3. Mind
A fuller view of God
We can and should engage our minds fully in pursuit of rest in God. I have talked much about emotion and embrace that certainly does not exclude our intellect. We need all our heart, soul, mind and strength to follow God wholeheartedly, and so we are called to renew our minds

---

[111] See 'Breathing' in the appendix.

in line with what we have been talking about. To read, listen and educate, allowing God to 'reprogramme' our minds is good and to be encouraged! Romans 12:2 calls us to renew our minds. God is not impersonal but has deliberately enabled us to know Him in our hearts, souls and minds! It was astronomist Johannes Kepler (1571–1630) who is widely acknowledged as saying that science is merely 'thinking God's thoughts after Him'.[112] Intellectually we can and should want to understand God, as much as we are able with our finite minds.

Catherine LaCugna, in her rather academic book *God for Us*, about God's willingness to come alongside and to be known by us, says:

> God is not an impersonal substance over and against the creature, a being tied to self that subjugates and dominates the creature, nor a being whose primary love is self-love. The God who does not need nor care for the creature or is immune to our suffering, does not exist. The God too hidden for us to know, or too powerful to evoke anything but fear, does not exist. The God who watches us from a distance as an uninvolved impartial observer, does not exist. The God conceived as a self-enclosed, exclusively self-related triad of persons, does not exist. The God who keeps a ledger of our sins and failings, the divine policeman, does not exist. These are all false gods, fantasies of the imagination that has allowed itself to become detached from the rule of God's life disclosed in

---

[112] www.cis.org.uk/wp-content/uploads/2015/02/01-Thinking-Gods-Thoughts-after-Him.pdf (accessed 4th April 2025).

Jesus Christ. What we believe about God must match what is revealed of God in Scripture; God watches over the widow and the poor, God makes the rain fall on just and unjust alike, God welcomes the stranger and embraces the enemy.[113]

We can know God as He has made Himself known, and that involves our minds. This may reframe our understanding of how we see the universe, understand the gospel and trust this loving God in whom we can find rest.

Waymarker pause
Does the above passage change how you think about or understand God? What have you considered God to be like in the past? Does this change or challenge your thinking?

4. Strength
Countering scarcity
I read recently that economics is the science of how people deal with scarcity.[114] We are fearful that there is a lack of resources, time and 'stuff'! Stuffocation is a recent phenomenon where we in the West hoard so much 'stuff' that our economy is based on it.[115] We are fearful of lack and scarcity with not enough to go round, so we need to grab what we can when and where we can. Many wealthy people now have so many possessions that they are

---

[113] Catherine LaCugna, *God for Us: The Trinity & Christian Life*, New York: HarperCollins Publishers, 1993 p 395.
[114] Peter Antonioni, *Economics for Dummies*, 2nd edition, 2010, Hoboken, NJ: John Wiley & Sons, 2010.
[115] James Wallman, *Stuffocation: Living More with Less*, London: Penguin, 2015.

turning to experiences as gifts, such as holidays, cruises, trekking and sports car events – and now we are so time-poor that we need experiences to make the best use of it. FOMO is a real problem in the West – Fear Of Missing Out – driven by the fear that we may miss out on some experience or something that we may need but never knew we needed!

I see this in Christian circles where I have witnessed a frenetic drive to attend as many events and watch as many YouTube sermons as possible, to absorb as much as we can because there might just be something we may be missing out on. This is certainly not a picture of people at peace or rest, knowing that a loving Father will not withhold any good thing from us.[116] That was part of the original temptation in the garden, sowing the seeds of doubt in God's goodness, that God was holding back on Adam and Eve. The fear of scarcity runs very deep, but the Father's abundant loving embrace counteracts that.

In a worldview based on scarcity, there is little room for our neighbour as we need to grasp what is scarce at the expense of others. To counteract this is to rest in the Father's embrace, knowing that no good thing that He has ordained for us will be lost. Do we trust our heavenly Father enough to stop our frenetic activity and to rest?

Sabbath rest

The Sabbath is a pause that permits us to reflect on who we are and who we are called to be; an opportunity to circle back on our identity, our faith and our humanity. Again, we take this back to the prodigal son, as the

---

[116] Psalm 84:11.

younger and older sons both knew the voice of scarcity, of not having enough, and they were always wanting more. We know it was a lie but still they swallowed it hook, line and sinker! The younger son stilled that voice forever in his father's embrace.

We can even bring this to bear on our idea of what is enough in terms of sacrifice. We are so driven by scarcity that even with God we feel we need to add more and more to our sacrifice to and for Him. God has said, 'Enough!' The cross covers it all; there is nothing more to pay. Stop, trust and rest. Unbelief can so often look like us running around trying to please God by being so busy for Him! Leviticus is a wonderful book where God quantifies in detail what is required in sacrifice. There is a tendency in many of us to always feel the need to do more, while God has said what is needed and, in the cross, paid it all.

Waler Bruggeman in his book *Sabbath as Resistance: Saying No to the Culture of Now* notes how Sabbath can be seen as resistance.[117] Sabbath rest is the longest commandment detailing fully and precisely who it is for. It is a wholesale requirement for a healthy human community, and if it's not observed, they will go back to the economy of Pharaoh. The first commandment says, 'I am … God, who brought you out of Egypt' (Exodus 20:1) which is a sharp contrast to Pharaoh's economy and defining narrative.

Forgo the Sabbath commandment and we very soon forget what it is to be the emancipated people of God. To live in God's embrace we need to practise the Sabbath. It

---

[117] Walter Bruggeman, *Sabbath as Resistance: Saying No to the Culture of Now*, Louisville, KY: Westminster John Knox Press, 2014.

is no longer a specific day,[118] but an attitude of heart and mind. Taking time out regularly as an act of resistance does no harm! You can do this as a day, a retreat, or even finding a quiet place you can go to. Charles Wesley's mother, Susanna, in a very busy house with lots of children running around, used to pull her shawl over her head, and that was her place of rest.[119]

Performance
Sabbath rest happily releases us from the slave driver of needing to perform, which many of us feel. I don't know if you have felt, as I have, that nagging, anxious feeling as you wake in the morning that there is so much to do and that so much could go wrong, that you must work, and work hard. Sabbath, among other gifts from God, is a release from that performance mentality. I find that when anxiety overloads me, I use it to drive me to Jesus, where I always find rest in prayer and Scripture.

These are just some examples that come to my mind, but I hope that you will know and learn from others as you explore the Father's embrace.

Waymarker pause
Sit and reflect, thinking about where you are trying to perform in your faith. What things cause you anxiety or fear, and drive you to keep 'the plates spinning' in your life?

You may want to speak to a trusted friend who will bring light and life to your fears and anxiety, rather than

---

[118] Colossians 2:16-17.
[119] www.faithgateway.com/blogs/christian-books/leaving-a-legacy-of-prayer-praying-example-susanna-wesley (accessed 5th April 2025).

compound them. Choose your confidant carefully – pick one who knows this rest.

Summary

God calls us to a rest that is both practical and tangible, one that can be experienced in at least four areas, reflecting Jesus' call for us to love with all our heart, soul, mind and strength. To experience this rest in these areas, we may need to take intentional steps to make it a reality. Each of these areas will resonate differently for each of us, depending on our unique situations and needs.

Waymarker

I have put a Waymarker pause after each of the areas covered, allowing you to stop at that point if it has moved you in a particular way.

Sit
Find that comfortable place where you can let your heart, soul, mind and body relax.

Reflect
Of all that you have read in this chapter, what one thing has struck you most? What do you want to do about it? What help do you need to do this?

Pray
The first step is to bring what you are feeling into the light of God's love. Bring these thoughts and feelings to God, trusting Him with them.

12
Cycle of grace

> I do not understand the mystery of grace – only that it meets us where we are and does not leave us where it found us.
> *Anne Lamott*[120]

Adam, at creation, needed to start on the correct foot, in the right attitude, to keep in step with God and His creational principles. We are encouraged to live by the Spirit and 'keep in step with the Spirit' (Galatians 5:25).

When we learn to begin from a place of acceptance and embrace, one of the key aspects of walking in step with the Spirit is that our lives and attitudes play out in a completely different way than when we try to find acceptance and value through our own efforts.

We have seen that there are fundamentally two yokes that we can carry, one yoke being the yoke of work, the burden of trying to navigate life through our own efforts and to find acceptance and worth through what we do; the other yoke is, of course, one of grace, where we find that acceptance and worth through God's gracious and loving embrace.

---

[120] www.brainyquote.com/quotes/anne_lamott_391308 (accessed 5th April 2025).

Two approaches

Here are two approaches to life which demonstrate the different yokes and life views we can live by.

The cycle of works[121]

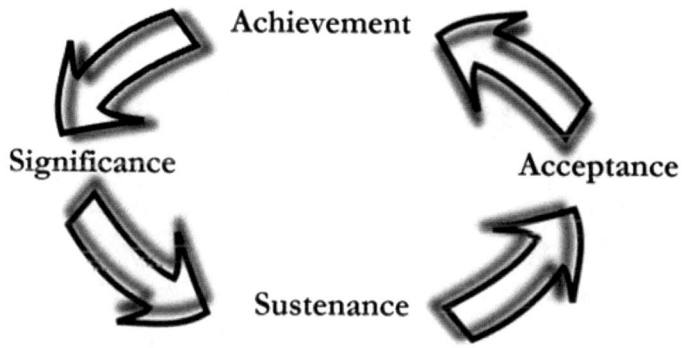

This cycle starts with achievement, working to attain something, and from that accomplishment comes our significance. We are what we have made ourselves to be by our own work. The next step in this cycle is to sustain this significance, which of course must be by more achievement. This explains the drivenness of many people; even when we are at the top of our particular ladder, it is never enough. So many high achievers and celebrities acknowledge this, yet we never learn. When we

---

[121] The 'Cycle of Grace' is said to originate from Dr Frank Lake and Dr Emil Brunner. This and the next diagram are adapted from www.novo.org/discipleship-blog/living-in-the-cycle-of-grace-the-confession-of-a-burned-out-missionary and also the website www.lovelitegivingwater.com/identity/understanding-the-cycle-of-grace which gives more information (accessed 23rd April 2025).

finally manage to sustain this ever-demanding hunger for achievement, we can at last feel accepted; but it is a fragile acceptance totally reliant on our efforts, which can be lost in a moment, so the insatiable cycle continues.

The cycle of grace

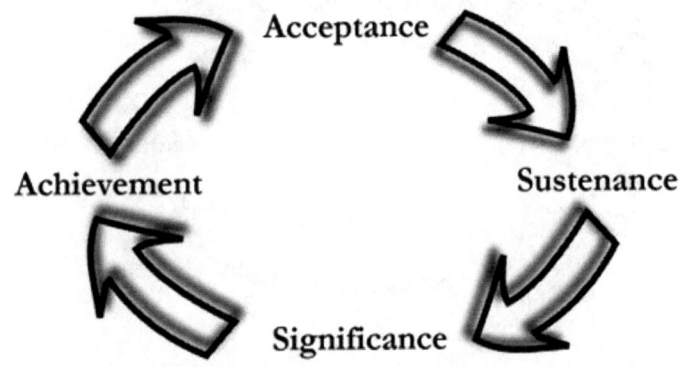

In this cycle, we start from the place of acceptance. This is the place of the Father's embrace and, of course, of Jesus' yoke. We are unconditionally accepted and loved and our task is to live into that, learning how to find sustenance in it and also sustaining that vital life-giving relationship, just as Jesus did. There is no drivenness here, but quiet acceptance. From this, we find our significance. Not based on what I can do or achieve but on who I am as a child of God, simply accepted, of incredible worth. That is who I am and that is where my significance lies. And from that wonderful, life-giving, secure platform, we can go to work and achieve. This is the place where Adam and Eve started their life on earth, and where the returning prodigal re-engaged in the family business. This is where Jesus calls us to a fresh start.

This reflects our earlier discussion about the true self and the false self. The false self feeds off and lives on the idea of achievement, while the resting true self knows it is accepted and starts from that secure footing. Many of us, including, and maybe especially, many pastors and 'full-time workers',[122] start well in the cycle of grace but slip into the cycle of works and need to meet expectations to find their significance.

Something to live for: the mission of rest

We have seen that Jesus is inviting us into His rest and His embrace. Those wonderful words from Matthew 11 begin to come alive, 'Come to me, all you who are weary' (v28), reflecting the invitation from Isaiah and echoing the original creation intent of rest:

> Come, all you who are thirsty,
> come to the waters;
> and you who have no money,
> come, buy and eat!
> Come, buy wine and milk
> without money and without cost.
> (Isaiah 55:1)

God knew fully what was to come. He knew of the anguish, pain and futility that would ensue before His creation work was finally completed in the new creation

---

[122] Though I dislike the term, as none of us is part-time in God's kingdom, I use it simply because it's commonly understood. I mean those generally supported or paid for their work in the church.

of the new heaven and earth. At the outset, God established beyond doubt the reality that He would be victorious, providing the solution before we even knew there was a problem. We are invited into this wonderful relationship so that we can invite others.

The world is desperate for that oxygen of freedom and hope; a true freeing from the confining slavery we all know as individual members of humanity. So many ways have been devised to break this yoke off us, but only Jesus has cut right through it by coming from a completely different perspective and in gaining a freedom that can only be known in Him. We are commissioned to bring that good news.

How do you find this?

I have spoken of my own journey into the Father's embrace, of knowing Jesus' yoke as a living reality in my life, but that is my journey. I cannot tell you how you should or will encounter Jesus, but I do know that if you come to Him, He will never turn you away.[123] Maybe you could start by simply speaking to Him and asking Him to show you what this means for you. Then, of course, you need to be willing and give time to listen. I suggest that you will need to slow down and learn to listen to your heart and to the Spirit.

One person's gift is another person's yoke

We have looked at possible different practices which you can explore and hopefully make your own, but we must

---

[123] John 6:37.

be careful not to take on something that can be unhelpful and a backward step. There are many ways this can happen, but here is an example to make you aware of how subtly it can creep up.

I recall attending a course on prayer, which promoted the need to pray for an hour every morning. I was working long hours, but nonetheless signed up, and each morning I would get up early – but our baby would wake up correspondingly early. I tried an hour earlier each morning until it got ridiculous, and eventually I had to give up, and so I felt a real failure. It was years before I could shake off this feeling of failure and be reconciled to the God who loves me not for what I do, but for who I am.

I fully agree with the need to pray, and have organised and led many prayer times, but in this call to an hour of prayer each morning, I was responding to someone else's expectations and experience, not God's voice to me – their yoke and not God's. I have come to recognise something Peter Wagner in his book, *Your Spiritual Gifts Can Help Your Church Grow*, calls 'gift projection',[124] which is when someone has a particular gift or ministry, and in humility correctly see themselves as nothing special. The thinking then goes, 'If I do this and this is my experience, and I am nothing special, then everyone else should also feel and do the same.' Thus they project their own calling and gifting onto others. For those who do not have this particular gift and are not secure in their own gifting, a feeling of guilt can easily follow.

---

[124] C Peter Wagner, *Your Spiritual Gifts Can Help Your Church Grow*, Ventura, CA: Regal Books, 1994, p 70.

We know that the Spirit gives separate gifts and empowers individuals differently so the body of Christ can work diversely but in unity. Wagner notes that in his research he has found that about 10 per cent of people have the gift of intercession, with the majority being women. We must be careful that we don't assume that if I am gifted in such and such a way, then everyone else should also feel and do the same. The yoke that was placed on me was someone else's expectations and experience, not my own, or God's for me.

Summary

God's rest is practical and can be applied practically to our lives. A challenge is not only to give mental assent to this idea but to actually begin to live into it. Rest can be found and applied to the four areas Jesus talks about – heart, soul, mind and strength. Our lives are either based on the belief that we must work for our acceptance, as our significance is derived from what we do, or alternatively on the belief that we are accepted as we are and in Christ we find out who we truly are, with our significance flowing from that.

Waymarker

Sit
Find that place of stillness in your heart where you can consider what your core motivations in life are.

Reflect
Is your life based on the cycle of works or the cycle of grace? Explore that and then consider quietly different

aspects of rest in heart, soul, mind and strength. Which one do you find most challenging, or is there another area that comes to mind?

Pray
Give your thoughts to God, and ask Him to work in your heart to teach you the way of rest.

13
In my end is my beginning

> We shall not cease from exploration
> And the end of all our exploring
> Will be to arrive where we started
> And know the place for the first time.
> *T S Eliot*[125]

I was sixteen years old and part of the school Christian Union, when for one Thursday lunchtime meeting, as I was preparing for my turn to lead the group, I was struggling for inspiration in what to say, and was praying for some sort of an idea. The hymn 'I Heard the Voice of Jesus Say' came to mind and I decided that a simple talk explaining and applying the verses in this hymn was what was called for. To the consternation of the others in the group, I was late to the meeting, which would normally have had about ten of us attending, but as I walked in, I saw all the seats in the classroom were taken and people sitting on desks. I have no idea how many there were that lunchtime, but I would guess around forty.

---

[125] www.goodreads.com/quotes/644987-we-shall-not-cease-from-exploration-and-the-end-of (accessed 5th April 2025).

I heard the voice of Jesus say,
'Come unto Me and rest;
Lay down, O weary one, lay down
Thy head upon My breast.'
I came to Jesus as I was,
Weary, and worn, and sad;
I found in him a resting-place,
And He has made me glad.

I heard the voice of Jesus say,
'Behold I freely give
The living water; thirsty one,
Stoop down, and drink, and live.'
I came to Jesus, and I drank
Of that life-giving stream;
My thirst was quench'd, my soul revived,
And now I live in Him.

I heard the voice of Jesus say,
'I am this dark world's Light;
Look unto me, your morn shall rise,
And all your day be bright.'
I looked to Jesus, and I found
In him my Star, my Sun;
and in that Light of life I'll walk,
Till trav'ling days are done.[126]

That was part of a remarkable time at school when we saw an awakening, with nothing short of a miraculous move of God touching many lives. It was in the intimate touch of

---

[126] Horatius Bonar (1808–89).

God and His invitation to come and rest that we experienced something remarkable.

I realise that in recalling this event, a large part of my life's journey has been to gradually grow in knowing this rest. If you care to stop, pray and listen, reflecting on your life's journey up to now, I think you too will find God's voice calling you, in His unique way, to a closer intimacy of rest in Him. Your heart may have ached, knowing that there was more to this Christian life but never quite grasping what it was. If what you have read in this book has spoken to you, as 'deep calls to deep' (Psalm 42:7), then this may be what you have been longing for, this union in a deeper, life-giving and life-affirming way.

This closer intimacy of rest which you long for may be much bigger than you dare think:

> 'What no eye has seen,
> what no ear has heard,
> and what no human mind has conceived' –
> the things God has prepared for those who love him.
> (1 Corinthians 2:9)

The weight of glory

In drawing to an end, I leave you with the most far-reaching image of God's infinite grace and His purpose for us, for you and me, taken from C S Lewis' sermon *The Weight of Glory*.[127] To paraphrase, it's not how we think of God that matters, but much more how He thinks of us. One day we will all stand before Him and, rather than

---

[127] Lewis, *The Weight of Glory*, p 38.

fearing His gaze, we should be amazed by His promise of glory. This promise of glory, which is only possible through the work of Christ, is that we will find not only God's approval but also the pleasure of being loved by Him. Lewis goes on to say that God does not simply pity us, but takes delight in us – and this divine delight is a glimpse of His purpose for us: the glory He intends to share. It is almost beyond comprehension, yet whether we grasp it fully or not, it remains true.

When I read about this weight, I was deeply struck again by the words of Jesus:

> Come to me, all you who are weary and burdened, and I will give you rest. Take my yoke upon you and learn from me, for I am gentle and humble in heart, and you will find rest for your souls. For my yoke is easy and my burden is light.
> (Matthew 11:28-30)

The yoke Jesus promises is not only for now but is also a promise for what is to come.

To rule and reign

It is wonderful to realise that the radiant splendour the Father wishes to bestow upon those who believe is this: to stand before Him in glory, not trembling in dread, but overflowing with joy in His love. Furthermore, not only will we stand before Him, but as part of that glory we are promised that we will rule and reign with Him in Christ![128] We can go back to the very beginning of creation, finding

---

[128] 2 Timothy 2:12; Revelation 5:10.

that God's original creational intention for humanity is glory. This ruling and reigning has always been part of the divine plan, and as God restores what has been lost to a better place than before, we will be part of something bigger and more glorious. From the fractured and fallen place we currently find ourselves in, we cannot fully conceive what this will be like, but we are assured it will be magnificent!

It has been quite a journey, but the promise is clear, that 'he who began a good work in you will carry it on to completion until the day of Christ Jesus' (Philippians 1:6).

How can we comprehend this? The yoke that Jesus calls us to, which as we have seen is the Father's embrace, is for God to delight in us. And an intrinsic part of the delight of God in us is that we will rule and reign with Him! How can this be? Whether or not we can grasp this does not matter, for whatever we think, it remains true. It is God who has planned this from before the creation of the world and it is God who has called us in Christ to be part of it. It is God from beginning to glorious end. Our part is to say, along with Mary, 'Behold, I am the servant of the Lord; let it be to me according to your word' (Luke 1:38, ESV).

That original rest from which Adam and Eve were created to rule the earth has been fully restored. In that full restoration of humanity to this place of rest, creation itself will also find rest. By grace in Christ, we have been restored to that original place of stewardship and rule. This fits with the idea we saw earlier when thinking about the pearl of great price. This pearl, representing you and me, is sought after, bought at great cost and then added to God's 'royal diadem' and 'crown of splendour' (Isaiah 62:3), the emblems of His rule and reign.

In this journey we have made together through these pages, we have only just touched on God's grace and what He has planned for us. I want this to have been a window to help you see fresh things in Scripture and God's powerful embrace for you. From here, may you continue in your journey into the Father's embrace, seeing new things and knowing in greater depth His love for you. In many ways, this is just the beginning. My prayer for you is that you would know this peace of Christ, not just in your head but also increasingly deeply in your body, heart, soul and mind. May it transform your life.

Waymarker

Sit
Find that place which I hope you are now familiar with to be at peace.

Reflect
As we come to the end of our journey together with this breathtaking final revelation of God's plan for us, what is your heart saying to you?

Prayer
Echo those wonderful words of Mary when she realised that God was wanting to do something in and through her, but it was too much for her to grasp: 'Let it be to me according to your word.'

14
A new story

> It is not the years in your life that count. It's the life in your years.
> *Edward J Stieglitz*[129]

A new story

As a Christian, the past no longer determines your future. The whole movement of Scripture is towards the new creation where God's rule and reign will be complete. The Lord's Prayer reflects this forward focus and movement, beginning with the request that God's 'will be done, on earth as it is in heaven' (Matthew 6:10) and finishing with His being the power and glory for ever.[130] We are caught up in this forward-looking progression, with our own needs of forgiveness and provision being met in the context of God's glory and plan. It does not begin or end with us. God's plan for your life and the future He has secured for you is what determines your future, not your past. In Christ we have been set free from the past.

---

[129] www.quoteinvestigator.com/2012/07/14/life-years-count (accessed 5th April 2025).

[130] In some late manuscripts (NIV).

The traditional thinking of a rabbi's yoke was their interpretation and application of the Mosaic Law. Jesus brings a completely different interpretation, which sets us free. Peter, as we know, let Jesus down badly when he denied Him three times, with the others, except John, running away. Peter was restored without a word of rebuke from Jesus.[131] Jesus did not need to rebuke him as Peter was keenly aware of what he had done – especially after he had promised to follow Him unconditionally. Jesus handled Peter's failure by loving him and calling him forward. We don't know whether Jesus physically embraced Peter, but He certainly did metaphorically. The future determined Peter's present, not his past.

Jesus' interpretation of His 'yoke' was one of grace and welcome, just the same as we see in the father's response to the returning son. Jesus talked about it, He taught it, He told stories about it and He did it. I don't think you can get more emphatic than that! And, of course, He calls us to do the same. We think, and the enemy tells us, that our past failures disqualify us from ministry, leadership, any kind of Christian service and even being part of God's family. As someone who has trusted in Jesus and taken His yoke upon me, I know that is a lie. In my view, failure can actually qualify us, as we understand from experience that we cannot do anything for God in our own strength, but in His infinite wisdom and grace He has allowed us to learn an invaluable lesson. That is a gift of such worth, not to be squandered or taken lightly.

Over the years I have often used a phrase to encourage those who feel too broken to be used by God: 'Never trust

---

[131] Matthew 26; John 21.

anyone who doesn't walk with a limp.' We all have failed, we all walk with a limp and we all need Jesus the rabbi, our Lord and Saviour, to place His yoke of loving embrace on us. This most certainly is not *carte blanche* permission to do whatever we want to, damaging whoever gets in the way in the process and yet expecting full restitution and qualification in return. Dietrich Bonhoeffer calls that 'cheap grace'.[132]

Redeeming our story

In her book, *Rising Strong*, Brené Brown[133] notes that we all need a story of some sort to make sense of life, and that we are hardwired for it. She goes on to say that if we own our story, we can write our own ending; if we deny the story, it owns us and gets to write the ending. The prodigal son came to his senses and took ownership of his life and his life story, deciding to come home.

Brown talks of a process of when we realise that something is not quite right. First, 'recognise' that something is wrong; second, 'rumble' (wrestle with that feeling until we work out what has just happened and why); and third, the 'revolution', when we take what we have learned and use it to change our perceptions and life. This is what we have been trying to do by using those Waymarkers.

God gives us an opportunity to take ownership of our story. We can do this by deciding to give it to God and

---

[132] Dietrich Bonhoeffer, *The Cost of Discipleship*, London: SCM Press, 2001, p 3.
[133] Brené Brown, *Rising Strong*, London: Penguin Random House, 2015.

allowing ourselves to be embraced and to take His yoke upon us. This radically changes what our story can look like, as we are no longer victims of circumstances, but by taking ownership can know God working out His purposes, in and through it. It changes my story to no longer being a victim of past circumstances, be it of my own or others' doing, but to a future-orientated story.

Not only does it change my life story but it also changes the story of creation, in which we find ourselves.

Brian McLaren comments that we are part of, and find ourselves in, the unfolding story of creation.[134] Not only are we placed in this story, but we also find ourselves in it, meaning we find out who we are, our identity and our purpose when we find the God of this story. We have a new, defining story to live by, which is one of restoration, as God says 'See, I am doing a new thing' (Isaiah 43:19). God gives all of us an opportunity to redefine who we are, our life's story and so our destiny.

In the parable of the prodigal we see God writing the story, as the father does not dismiss the son but is always looking and hoping for his return. To 're-story' our lives is to take that perspective shown in the Lord's Prayer, which starts with 'Our Father' and ends with His kingdom, power and glory. We have a tendency to make the story about us, putting ourselves at the beginning, middle and end, while it is not our story at all. God writes the story of creation, not just us; history is His-story. We look at it from our perspective, but to change perspectives and see it from the Father's brings life, hope and peace. Back in Genesis

---

[134] Brian McLaren, *The Story We Find Ourselves In: Further Adventures of a New Kind of Christian*, San Francisco, CA: Josey-Bass, 2003.

15, we saw God working in the story through one man believing in Him, a story that started in Genesis 1 and runs through to Revelation 22 This is the narrative in which we find ourselves, in the sense of both our situation and our identity. By allowing yourself to take on Jesus' yoke and to be embraced by the Father you are recognising that it is His story and that you can begin to rest, as it's not about you at all!

God's gift to us is a new life story with a glorious new ending.

Conclusion

The book *Poet & Peasant* by Kenneth Bailey that I referred to earlier shows that the parable of the prodigal son is poetry that has a clear structure and stanzas. Jesus deliberately left off the last line, which would have been a very obvious and uncomfortable omission to the listeners. This omission would automatically engage the listener in trying to work out the missing last line to complete the story and balance the structure. Did the older son come to the celebration, or did he stay alone, angry in the field? Jesus posed this as a question for the Pharisees and all the listeners, to answer for themselves.

As Jesus challenged them to respond, I wonder how we will respond to this message and Jesus' call to take His yoke upon us? I trust that heaven is where we want to be,[135] and will finally allow ourselves to be fully embraced.

---

[135] Heaven is not the place of clouds and fat cherubs playing harps, but the place where we with all creation will finally and fully be fulfilled. Our life here is merely the smallest taste of the life to come, in which will be the full banquet!

We may be fearful we will lose our individuality, but in reality, we will find it. Part of our fallen nature is our independence and individuality which, when redeemed, is given up to God, and in doing so, we find ourselves.

Will you submit to the Father's embrace and seek greater intimacy with Him, or will you stubbornly continue in the wooden yoke of work and isolation? It's your call.

Waymarker

Sit

As we have done before, find a quiet place where you can reflect in an unhurried way.

Reflect

How do you see your life's story? What is the story you have written for yourself? Is it based on your failures, your shortcomings or on what has happened to you? What do you think is the different life story and ending that God is writing for you?

Prayer

Lord,
Through fresh realisation of Your tender, undeserved, loving embrace,
May my heart be softened and my life transformed.
Help me to discover new meaning and purpose
Through a deeper understanding of You and of myself.
May Your peace rule in my heart and, in Your embrace, renew the story of my life.
Draw me closer, restore what has grown distant,

And let me find fresh hope and joy in Your presence.
As I grow in Your love, may it shape how I see You, see myself
And see others, and how I walk through the world around me.
Lord, I ask that I may know and live in Your grace more deeply each day –
Today, and in all the days to come.
Amen.

Appendix

Breathing

A quick guide to what I mean by 'breathing', which I have learned over time and is my own practice. Feel free to explore for yourself as there is a lot of good Christian-based material available.

Simply find a quiet place, then pray, committing this time to God, asking the Spirit to guide you and Jesus to speak to you.

Breathe slowly and deeply. For instance, try breathing in for a count of four and out for a count of six or eight. Another way is to practise square breathing: breathe in for a count of two or three, hold it, let it go and then wait before breathing in, thinking of each stage as a side of a square. When you get used to breathing in this way, it becomes more automatic so you don't have to concentrate. Begin to notice what may come to your senses, reflecting these back to God in silent prayer.

There is nothing 'magical' about breathing deeply; it just helps your mind and body to relax. Very simply put, as you breathe deeply and slowly, you are sending powerful messages to your mind and body to say that 'I am safe'.

When we stop, so often regrets of the past or fear of the future come flooding in, but we can make a conscious decision, just for the moment, to be in the present, trusting in God's forgiveness of the past and provision for the future.

Sitting

I have learned to sit with Jesus. I don't do it often enough, but when I do I sit in a comfortable chair in a quiet space. I ask Jesus to come and be with me and then I simply sit. Often, I imagine myself being enfolded by God's grace and let myself go into this loving embrace.

At times Jesus will speak to me through an unexpected thought or feeling; sometimes He doesn't, but the aim is to give fifteen minutes or so just to sit in His company and open my heart to His presence. It is up to Him what He does with this time!

We all struggle with wandering thoughts, so don't be put off by them, but simply come back to breathing, reminding yourself of God's embrace and asking the Holy Spirit to guide you.

It can help to be with people who can walk with you in this, as the Celtic Church knew with their term 'anamcara', meaning someone who walks with you, or a soul friend. A retreat can help you deliberately set time aside to go to a place which is conducive to prayer and reflection. Where this place is and how you use it can vary greatly.[136] Many find it helpful to engage in a retreat, as it gives space and time to find Jesus in an unhurried way, with temporary relief from the usual stresses and strains of life.

---

[136] To find a place of retreat, see www.retreats.org.uk/findaretreat (accessed 6th April 2025). This is not an exhaustive list and there are other similar sites.

A simple spiritual discipline like Lectio Divina can be helpful (see next section). The main thing is to find a rhythm that works for you and get into the way of it.

Lectio Divina

Lectio Divina (Latin for 'Divine Reading') is a traditional monastic practice of scriptural reading, meditation and prayer intended to promote communion with God and to increase the knowledge of God's Word. It does not treat Scripture as texts to be studied, but as the living Word. Traditionally, Lectio Divina has four separate steps: read; meditate; pray; contemplate. First a passage of Scripture is read, then its meaning is reflected upon. This is followed by prayer and contemplation. The focus of Lectio Divina is not a theological analysis of biblical passages but to view them with Christ as the key to their meaning.[137]

A loving embrace for all.

While I was speaking about 'the Father's embrace' at a conference, a lady asked if I could express it another way. She explained that, sadly, she had never experienced an embrace like that. This is the reality for so many – never having known the warmth of a loving or accepting embrace of any kind. Her question prompted me to consider how I might convey this idea in a way she, and others with similar experiences, could connect with. I offered the following explanation that she said was helpful.

---

[137] www.ignatianspirituality.com/ignatian-prayer/the-what-how-why-of-prayer/praying-with-scripture (accessed 5th April 2025). This is just an example as there are many similar sites.

A loving and accepting embrace may be like how a mother holds her newborn child. Or, in another image, to use Jesus' own words, 'as a hen gathers her chicks under her wings' (Matthew 23:37). There is a lovely story of a mother hen shielding her young chicks from a hawk flying overhead when she calls them to herself and gathers them under her wings to protect them from danger.[138] In using this powerful image in the Gospel of Matthew, echoing Psalm 91:4, Jesus offers a tender and accessible expression of God's loving embrace.

---

[138] www.peggyjoyceruth.org/how-a-mother-hen-protectors-her-baby-chicks---psalm-91/how-a-mother-hen-protectors-her-baby-chicks-psalm-91 (accessed 14th May 2025).

Looking to go deeper?

A six-week study guide is available to accompany this book. To find out more or to contact Chic, please visit chiclidstone.com.